THE
BARRY RAILWAY

D. S. BARRIE

THE OAKWOOD PRESS

The pages and illustrations in this book are numbered in series with the same author's previous books in the Oakwood Library, " The Taff Vale Railway " (pages 1 to 44), " The Rhymney Railway " (pages 45 to 92), and " The Brecon and Merthyr Railway " (pages 93 to 150).

© *D. S. Barrie, 1962*
Printed by The Campfield Press, St. Albans
and published by The Oakwood Press
in March, 1962
Reprinted August, 1978
Reprinted with additions 1983
ISBN 0 85361 236 6

THE BARRY RAILWAY

IN size and importance the Barry Railway ranked second only to its neighbour and rival the Taff Vale among the independent railways which served the South Wales coalfield prior to the great railway amalgamations of the 1920s. It will long be remembered as one of the most efficient and most prosperous of the numerous local companies which competed for the coal and shipping trades, but, viewed in historical perspective, its significance becomes much more than local.

The Barry Railway was in fact both a symbol and a phenomenon: a symbol of the power and influence of the South Wales steam coal trade, which towards the end of the nineteenth century created new docks and railways almost overnight, and established around the oceans a chain of coaling stations serving most of the navies and mercantile marines of the world. The Barry was a symbol, too, of the ultimate expansion of railways in Great Britain. It was the last company to be incorporated among those which attained the dignity of being " constituents ", as distinct from " subsidiaries ", of the enlarged Great Western Railway Company in consequence of the Railways Act of 1921. Its only rival to the claim of being the last major independent railway company to be formed in Great Britain was the Hull & Barnsley, which was four years its elder, and was somewhat larger but less prosperous. The Barry was also notable as the largest example in these islands of a completely integrated dock-and-railway undertaking to be planned and constructed as such.

It was for what it accomplished in so short a time, and for the volume of traffic which it handled so remuneratively in so small a compass, that the Barry Railway may be regarded as a phenomenon. Its separate corporate existence was less than forty years (1884–1921), but in that period it

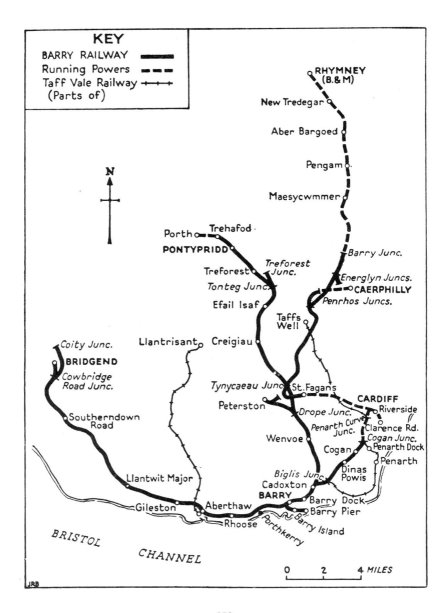

KEY

BARRY RAILWAY

Running Powers

Taff Vale Railway

(Parts of)

N

RHYMNEY
(B. & M)

New Tredegar

Aber Bargoed

Pengam

Maesycwmmer

Trehafod

Porth

PONTYPRIDD

Barry Junc.

Treforest
Junc.

Treforest

Energlyn Juncs.

CAERPHILLY

Tonteg Junc.

Penrhos Juncs.

Efail Isaf

Taffs
Well

Llantrisant

Creigiau

Coity Junc.

BRIDGEND

Cowbridge
Road Junc.

Tynycaeau Junc.

St. Fagans

CARDIFF

Peterston

Riverside

Southerndown
Road

Drope Junc.

Penarth Curve
Junc.

Clarence Rd.

Wenvoe

Cogan Junc.

Penarth Dock

Cogan

Penarth

Dinas
Powis

Llantwit Major

Biglis Junc

Cadoxton

BARRY

Gileston

Aberthaw

Barry Dock

Barry Pier

Rhoose

Porthkerry

Barry Island

BRISTOL

CHANNEL

0   2   4 MILES

JRB

152

grew from the daydream of a few courageous men to establish one of the finest coal ports in the country at which nearly 4,000 ships a year were dealt with in the boom years, and whose combined imports and exports often exceeded 10 or 11 million tons annually. Of 37 million tons of coal and coke shipped through South Wales ports in the record year (1913), more than 11 million tons were shipped through Barry—the greatest quantity of any port in the country. This was the zenith of the South Wales coal trade, and we shall never see its like again.

All this the Barry accomplished over a railway system which, with the inclusion of the subsidiary Vale of Glamorgan Railway (nominally an independent company but worked by the Barry), amounted to less than 68 route miles of line. But the total length of single track, including sidings, was over 300 miles, while with a stock of 148 locomotives (1921) the ratio of locomotives to route miles was greater than 2 to 1. Perhaps the most remarkable thing about the Barry, however, was that it handled this immense coal traffic while serving scarcely a single colliery direct; almost the entire coal traffic carried by the company was deftly abstracted from the neighbouring systems of the Taff Vale, Rhymney, Great Western, and Brecon & Merthyr Railways.

If coal was the mainstay—and was eventually to prove the weakness—of the Barry, the company was enterprising in sundry other directions: it operated a smart suburban service in and out of Cardiff; it largely created a popular holiday resort at Barry Island; and it was among the select group of British Railway companies that ran passenger steamers. But if success did come quickly, and to the tune of $9\frac{1}{2}$–10 per cent. dividends on the Ordinary stock during the last nine years of the company's life, it was not achieved without a tremendous initial struggle.

The Barry Dock & Railways came into existence because of the dissatisfaction of important coalowners and shippers at the inadequacy of rail and shipping facilities to cope with the rapid expansion of the coal trade in the latter part of the nineteenth century. The original and still the principal outlet for this trade, at the time this story opens, was Cardiff, whose development had been so rapid that it was already the third largest seaport in the United Kingdom, although in 1800 its population had been no more than 1,000. By 1850 the first railway proper (as distinct from tramroads) to serve the port of Cardiff was carrying 600,000 tons of coal a year; within ten years this figure was to rise to over 2 million tons. By arrangement with the Marquis of Bute, the Taff Vale Company used the Bute West Dock, while from 1858 onwards the adjacent Bute East Dock was used by the Rhymney Railway (originally a dependent, but later a rival of the Taff Vale) to bring down coal from the Rhymney Valley.

First Plans for a Port

Barry at this time was a rural village with a population of less than 100, and no hint among them that within a few decades it would become a thriving seaport, and eventually a borough with a population of 40,000. Its position eight miles south-west of Cardiff, with a good deep-water approach and the shelter afforded by Barry Island, was potentially ideal for a port, but hitherto it appears to have figured in maritime history only as the landing-place (actually on nearby Porthkerry Beach) of the Norman invaders of Wales; as the haunt of mediaeval pirates and later of smugglers; and in the eighteenth century as a haven of refuge for storm-bound ships. The principal event during the first half of the nineteenth century seems to have been the opening of the first boarding-house in 1811. The 1860s, however, were to see an initial and nearly successful attempt to establish a rail-served port at Barry, by means of a project which both in title and pattern approximated closely to the Barry Dock & Railways as eventually built.

It was in 1865—the year in which Penarth Dock was opened by a subsidiary company of the Taff Vale Railway in order to relieve congestion at Cardiff—that the first Barry Railway Company was incorporated, by Act of 5 July. The directors were headed by Sir Ivor Bertie Guest, Bart. (afterwards Lord Wimborne), the eldest son of Sir Josiah John Guest, the Dowlais ironmaster and first chairman of the Taff Vale Railway. The original Barry Railway Company was authorised to make a railway about 7 miles long from a junction with the G.W.R. South Wales main line at Peterston (between Cardiff and Llantrisant) to Cadoxton, with a branch thence to Sully; the main line was thus virtually the same as the Drope Branch of the Barry Dock & Railways authorised in 1884. The 1865 Act empowered the original Barry Company to complete and open its railway on either the 4 ft. 8½ in. or the 7 ft. gauge, whichever it preferred; but the formation was to be made wide enough for the broad gauge, and the G.W.R. was empowered to compel the laying of a third rail if it so desired. The two companies were also empowered to make agreements for the laying of a third (standard-gauge) rail over the G.W.R. between Peterston and Llantrisant on the west, and between Peterston, Cardiff, and Newport on the east, and for the Barry Company's use of the G.W.R. between these points. In the following year the original scheme was amended by two Acts which substituted a new route 8 miles long from Peterston to Barry (with the same provisions as to dual gauge); and a branch 3 miles long from Cadoxton to a junction with the Penarth Railway (T.V.R.). A third Act of 1866 incorporated the Barry Harbour Company, for converting the estuary of Barry Island into a tidal harbour, with powers for the Barry Railway Company to subscribe up to £9,000. Sir Ivor Guest was not named among the directors appointed under the Harbour Company's Act, and the only director of either the Railway Company or the Harbour Company to be actively associated with the Barry Dock & Railways nearly twenty years later was R. F. L. Jenner of Wenvoe Castle.

Nothing survived from these enactments of 1865–6 except the idea of a rail-connected port at Barry, and the powers were eventually abandoned by Board of Trade certificates in 1878–9, only five years before the incorporation of the Barry Dock & Railways Company. The reasons for this failure are not far to seek: the junction with the G.W.R. at Peterston offered only limited access to a then relatively unimportant part of the coalfield, and none to the Rhondda, Taff, and Aberdare valleys; the prospective working arrangement with the G.W.R. would be inimical to the Taff Vale, for these

twain loved not one another; while any traffic which the
T.V.R. might send to Barry via the Penarth connection
would only be at the expense of ports in which the Taff itself
was interested.   Finally, the financial crisis of 1866 effectively
stifled this and many other railways promoted at about that
time.

The Penarth, Sully & Barry Scheme

A second abortive attempt to extend railway communication to Barry was that of the Penarth, Sully & Barry
Railway Company, incorporated by Act of 2 August 1877 to
make a line 6 miles in length between the points named, in
connection with the Taff Vale's Penarth Railway.   The
moving spirit in this promotion was one Samuel Augustus
Tylke, who had secured a lease of land at Barry Island for
the purpose of developing it residentially and as a seaside
resort.   The Penarth, Sully & Barry was further authorised
by its Act of Incorporation to make working arrangements
with the Taff Vale, and according to Edgar L. Chappell's
History of the Port of Cardiff the T.V.R. took up the scheme but
withdrew its support in face of opposition by local landowners and by Cardiff and Penarth dock and shipping
interests.   Tylke's scheme therefore collapsed, and he
disposed of his land interests to Lord Windsor (afterwards
Earl of Plymouth), who was to become the first and only
chairman of the Barry Dock & Railways Company.   In
later years the Taff Vale management must have regretted
their decision to forsake the Penarth, Sully & Barry project,
because if the line had been built the Taff would have been
in control at Barry, and the coalowners who promoted the
Barry Dock & Railways Company only a few years later
would have been forced either to come to terms with the
Taff Vale or to make their intended dock and railway on a
less suitable location further west.

Although the Taff Vale had many pressing preoccupa-
tions at the time its withdrawal appears in retrospect all the
more surprising, because by then all the factors which were to
lead to the establishment of the Barry Dock & Railways were
dangerously plain to see.   Between 1873 and 1883 the coal

output of the Rhondda Valley alone rose from less than 2½ million to over 7 million tons a year, while between 1875 and 1883 shipments of coal and coke from Cardiff increased from less than 4 million to nearly 9 million tons a year. Yet during this period the only expansion of shipping facilities at Cardiff was the opening of Roath Basin in 1874. In that year the Bute Trustees had obtained powers to build a new Roath Dock, but did not proceed with it because they thought the expansion of the coalfield was already reaching its peak.

The congestion of shipping at Cardiff was such that not only were vessels sometimes kept outside for long periods waiting a berth, but those inside the docks were moored so close together that it was sometimes possible to walk from one side of the dock to the other across their decks. This was matched by the congestion on the Taff Vale Railway, on which it was alleged that trains stood head-to-tail for hours without turning a wheel, while frequently the collieries were stopped for lack of empty wagons. Since the Taff Vale Company's rates structure was so ingeniously contrived that the coalowners in the Rhondda (where the Taff had a complete monopoly) paid proportionately the highest rates, it was not surprising that the Rhondda proprietors combined together to overthrow the Bute–Taff Vale monopoly.

Their leader in this revolt was the redoubtable David Davies of Llandinam (1818–90), who after spending the early part of a crowded and successful life building railways in various parts of Wales, in 1865 had begun sinking pits in the Upper Rhondda. By 1884 the operations of the Ocean Collieries group, as it had become known, extended outside the Rhondda into the neighbouring Ogmore and Garw Valleys. For the greater part of a decade David Davies and his associates harried the Bute Trustees and the Taff Vale Railway to expand their facilities to meet the growth of coal traffic, and in 1877 he supported (but subsequently withdrew from) the projected Pontypridd, Caerphilly & Newport Railway, which was incorporated in 1878 and opened in 1884 to afford an alternative shipping outlet for Rhondda coal.

The dispute between the coalowners and shippers on the one hand and the Bute Trustees and Taff Vale Railway on

the other came to a head in 1882, when the Trustees brought
forward a Bill to revive the Roath Dock scheme, but
associated with it a proposal to charge an extra penny a ton
on coal shipped not only at the new dock, but at all the other
Bute Docks.   In bitterly contesting the proposed additional
charge, the freighters said in effect that if Roath Dock could
not be built without the extra charge, they would build a
new dock themselves, and David Davies told the House of
Commons Committee that " we have 5 million tons of coal,
and can fill a thundering good dock the first day we open it."

The Bills in Parliament

In fact, the first steps to revive the scheme for a port at
Barry had already been taken.   David Davies and his
associates had re-examined the earlier proposals in consulta-
tion with R. F. L. Jenner, and had preferred them to the
alternative site which had been suggested further west at the
mouth of the Ogmore River.   Even before the Bute Trustees
obtained their Act for the Roath Dock (with some modifications in regard to the increased charges), several meetings of
the prospective Barry promoters had been held, consulting
engineers engaged, and the support ensured of Lord
Windsor, Lord Romilly, and other landowners at and
around Barry.   Before the end of 1882 the Parliamentary
plans had been lodged and the Bill deposited for the incorporation of the Barry Dock & Railways Company.
    Despite the massive support which the project com-
manded from coalowners and shipping interests, the serried
opposition of the Bute Trustees, the Taff Vale and the
Rhymney Railway companies, and other vested interests
secured its defeat in the Parliamentary Session of 1883.   The
contest was renewed in the following Session after the Barry
faction had vainly offered to buy the Bute Docks as a gesture
of their confidence that there was room for both Cardiff and
Barry.   This particular Parliamentary battle has captured
the imagination of historians, and as it is fully recounted
elsewhere,* repetition in the present account seems needless;

* Notably in the *History of the Barry Railway Company, 1884–1921*, and in
Top Sawyer, by Ivor Thomas (Longmans, Green, 1938).

suffice it to say that after much telling evidence by David Davies and his adherents as to the cost of the delays to ships and to colliery-owned wagons at Cardiff, the Bill was passed and received the Royal Assent on 14 August 1884. The promoters' costs for the two Bills were about £70,000, and, for the first time on record, a special dispensatory clause enabled the costs of the unsuccessful Bill of 1883 to be charged to the company.

Thus was incorporated The Barry Dock & Railways Company, although the title did not long survive in this form. Because the precedence given to " Dock " over " Railways " required the shares to be dealt with as " docks " rather than " Home Rails ", and presumably in order to qualify for trustee status, the title was changed to The Barry Railway Company by Act of 5 August 1891; South Walians generally abridged it to " the Barry ", anyway. Its initial authorised capital was £1,050,000 in shares, with borrowing powers up to £350,000. Robert George Windsor-Clive, Lord Windsor (created Earl of Plymouth in 1905), was elected the first chairman and held that office from beginning to end of the Barry company's corporate life. David Davies was the first deputy chairman, although clearly he acted as unofficial " managing director " during the construction of the dock and railway; he was already 65 years of age at the incorporation and was destined barely to survive the fulfilment of his dream. Other notable directors at the outset were Crawshay Bailey, a famous pioneer of railways in South Wales and Monmouthshire, who died in 1887, and T. R. Thompson, a Cardiff shipping magnate who was a tower of strength to the company until his death in 1919. The first roll of directors was also strongly representative of coal-owning interests and included such famous names as Cory and Insole.

The railways authorised by the Act of Incorporation extended eastward from Barry to Cadoxton ($1\frac{3}{4}$ miles), whence the main line turned north through mainly undeveloped, rural country to a junction with the Rhondda branch of the Taff Vale Railway at Trehafod, $1\frac{1}{4}$ miles north of Pontypridd and $18\frac{3}{4}$ miles from Barry. From the main line, four short branches were authorised:

From Drope Junction, 4¾ miles from Cadoxton, for a distance
of 2 miles to join the G.W.R. main line at Peterston;

At Tynycaeau Junction,* 5¾ miles from Cadoxton, a connection
1 mile in length came up from the G.W.R. at St. Fagan's to trail
into the Barry line in a northward direction ;

At Creigiau, 8¾ miles from Cadoxton, a very short connection
was to be made to the Llantrisant & Taff Vale Railway's Waterhall
Junction–Common Branch Junction line which had been authorised
in 1866;

At Tonteg Junction, 12¼ miles from Cadoxton, a connection,
1¾ miles long, led down to join the Taff Vale main line at Treforest
Junction, for the purpose of drawing off traffic originating in the
Taff and Aberdare Valleys.

The railways thus authorised totalled about 23 miles and
were in the form of a tree-trunk with a few short branches.
In later years as the system grew, it took on the appearance
of an octopus with its head on the shore at Barry and its
tentacles stretching out north, east and west; the simile is by
no means inappropriate to a railway which drew off most of
its traffic from others. The system thus authorised in 1884
differed from that proposed in the previous year by omitting
the intended branch from Cadoxton to Penarth, and in being
cut short at the Trehafod Junction with the T.V.R., instead
of continuing up the Rhondda Valley, on the opposite side
of the river to the Taff Vale, to Cwmparc, where David
Davies had struck the main steam coal seam in 1866. The
Act of Incorporation required that the main line to Trehafod
was not to be brought into use before the connection with
the G.W.R. at St. Fagan's, but this was no hardship to the
Barry, who relied on this connection for getting materials and
equipment with which to build the line. The connection
which had been authorised with the Llantrisant & Taff Vale
(a T.V.R. subsidiary) where the two railways intersected
near Creigiau was never made, possibly because the coal
traffic from the Ely Valley could be tapped via the Drope–
Peterston connection with the G.W.R.

Despite David Davies's strongly expressed views against
working loaded coal trains uphill, it was impossible to avoid
this in laying out the Barry system, largely because it had to
connect out of existing railways which already held the

---

* The spelling of this and other place-names is that normally used by the
Barry company.

water-level routes along the river valleys. Thus, an initial climb at 1 in 220 was required to get out of the Rhondda Valley towards Pontypridd, where the Barry line was to pass through the western part of the town, close to, but at a higher level than, the Taff Vale. Thereafter nothing more severely against the engines than some stretches at 1 in 400 between Tynycaeau and Wenvoe would be met with on the way to Cadoxton, with descents at 1 in 120 and at 1 in 127 north of Tynycaeau and between Wenvoe and Cadoxton respectively. The gradients were only kept down to these inclinations, however, by some heavy and costly engineering, including the Treforest Tunnel of 1,373 yd. between Pontypridd and Treforest, and the Wenvoe Tunnel of 1 m. 108 yd., latterly the sixth longest in Wales, between Drope Junction and Wenvoe. There was also some extensive cutting work, two substantial bridges across the River Taff and some colliery lines respectively between Trehafod and Pontypridd, and the viaducts by which the railway was to be carried across the Ely River and the G.W.R. main line between Tynycaeau and Drope Junctions. The original branch lines included ascents of 1 in 89 between St. Fagan's and Tynycaeau Junction and of 1 in 101 from Treforest Junction up to the main line at Tonteg Junction.

Barry Dock

Engineering features of the railway system were overshadowed, however, by the spectacular work involved in the construction of Barry Dock itself, which was to be 73 acres in extent, the largest enclosed dock in the country; the total area between Barry Island and the mainland, from which tidal water had to be excluded, was some 200 acres. The dock was to be 3,400 ft. long and of 1,100 ft. maximum width, with a maximum depth of water of 37 ft. 9 in. at ordinary spring tides.

The engineers who supervised the work of construction were those who had drawn up the plans for the promoters: (Sir) John Wolfe Barry and his partner H. M. Brunel, and T. Forster Brown of Cardiff. Sir John Barry was to continue as a consultant and expert Parliamentary witness for the

Barry Company for some twenty years, while Brunel was the son of Isambard Kingdom Brunel, who incidentally had planned the largely parallel route of the Taff Vale Railway nearly half-a-century before. Another distinguished name associated with the construction of the Barry Railway was (Sir) James W. Szlumper, who had been engineer for the Pontypridd, Caerphilly & Newport Railway, and who now took charge of the northern section of the Barry main line. This included the Treforest Tunnel, at the Pontypridd portal of which was placed in the arch a stone plaque inscribed with the names of Szlumper and of T. A. Walker; the latter, who was also contractor for such famous works as the Severn Tunnel and the Manchester Ship Canal, built the northern section of the Barry main line under Szlumper's supervision.

The Taff renews the Battle

While the Barry directors thus busied themselves throughout the remainder of 1884 in their temporary offices at Cardiff with the letting of contracts, with promoting a successful public issue of shares, with planning for the raising of more capital to meet a total constructional cost for the dock and railways of about £2,000,000, and incidentally with the cutting of the first sod by Lord Windsor at Barry on 14 November 1884, fresh clouds of conflict were looming to dim for a spell the happy sunrise of initial triumph. The Taff Vale Railway might have lost the Parliamentary contest by a second-round knockout, but it soon showed its determination to renew the battle with the object of impeding and hampering the intruder in as many different directions as possible.

This warfare between the Barry and the Taff Vale was destined to go on, with varying intensity, for some thirty years, and it is important to appreciate the fundamental way in which it differed from most of the other inter-railway rivalries in South Wales. It was not merely that the Taff Vale, and to a lesser degree its neighbour the Rhymney Railway, were faced with the competition of a new *railway*, largely promoted and lavishly financed by coalowners who were already among the largest customers of the Taff Vale. The Taff and the Rhymney brought most of their shipment coal traffic to Cardiff Docks, but except that both companies had the use of certain coal-shipping appliances under agreement, they were unable to dictate either the expansion of the dock facilities or the scale of dock charges; moreover, the Taff Vale in particular had more than once quarrelled with the Bute Trustees (in whom the Cardiff Docks had been vested since 1845), notably in connection with the railway company's leasing of Penarth Dock, opened in 1865. No such difficulties were foreseen for the Barry Company, which as we have already seen was planned as an integrated dock-and-railway undertaking. The competition facing the Taff Vale and the Rhymney was therefore something much stronger than purely railway competition, and the older-established companies rightly appreciated that the Barry would enjoy not only the massive support of the traders themselves, but also the advantage of this dock-and-railway integration. Even twenty years later, when the Barry offered to act jointly with other companies in opening up a new route into the West Monmouthshire coalfield, the offer was rejected because its rivals were afraid that the Barry, by manipulation of its dock charges, would drive the proverbial coach-and-four through any joint agreement on railway rates. Thus the Barry was not just a horse of a different colour: it was an entirely different animal. Not unfittingly, its emblem* featured the Red Dragon " passant, wings addorsed ", with as crest a stag at gaze; the crest being from the armorial achievement of the Windsor-Clives.

One of the first moves made by the Taff Vale after the incorporation of the Barry Company was to seek to acquire the Bute Docks. The House of Lords Select Committee, however, was only prepared to pass the Taff's Bill promoted in the 1885 Session on condition that the Barry should be given running powers over the T.V.R. northward and westward of the two systems at Treforest; this the older company was not willing to do, and it withdrew its Bill. The two companies clashed on different grounds in the same Session

* As with most railway companies' armorial devices, this emblem appears to have had no heraldic authority.

when the Taff Vale supported the proposals of the nominally independent Cardiff, Penarth & Barry Junction Railway to build two lines: one from Penarth direct to Barry, and another round the coast by Lavernock and Sully, the latter being largely a revival of Tylke's abortive project of 1877. The greater threat to the Barry's peace of mind was the direct line from Penarth, which with seeming ingenuousness was planned to terminate on the site which the Barry had already earmarked for its No. 2 Dock! The Barry countered this threat by reviving its previous scheme for the branch from Cadoxton to Penarth, and appeared to emerge substantially the victor; for whereas the C. B. & P. got powers only for its coastal loop to join the B.R. at Biglis Junction, 32 ch. east of Cadoxton station, the Barry by its Act of 31 July 1885 was authorised to build its direct line $5\frac{1}{4}$ miles long, from Cadoxton to a junction at Cogan with the Penarth Extension Railway (the Penarth passenger branch of the T.V.R.).

The Coal Rates Battle

The Barry's immediate victory was more apparent than real, however, the snag being that the Taff Vale clearly intended as far as possible to haul coal originating on its system and destined for Barry Dock round the coastal loop to Biglis Junction, instead of handing it over to the Barry at the Hafod, Treforest, or Cogan junctions. Under existing legislation the Barry company's rate for coal from common points to Barry via Hafod or Treforest would have to be based on the T.V.R. rate over the longer distance via the coastal loop. While the local railways from Cadoxton to Cogan and Biglis to Penarth were under construction, battle was therefore joined again, on the issue of discriminatory rates. In the Parliamentary Session of 1888, the Barry applied for running powers over the Taff Vale northward and westward of Treforest. Although these were refused except as a penalty for possible non-compliance by the Taff Vale with the Barry Dock & Railways Act, 1888, Clause 23 of this Act required the Taff Vale to afford the Barry facilities for the exchange of goods and mineral traffic at

Treforest and Hafod, with no discrimination as to rates, which were not to be greater than the lowest T.V.R. rate to Cardiff, Penarth, or Barry. Moreover, save with the Barry's permission the Taff Vale was not to use the coastal loop to Biglis for mineral traffic other than purely local traffic, while the Taff Vale's running powers over Biglis Junction were limited to passenger trains, into Cadoxton station only.

With the strategic dispute between the two companies thus momentarily shelved, the junctions at Biglis and Cogan were opened simultaneously on 20 December 1888, although initially very little passed over them. The Barry was not ready to start any goods traffic, nor to operate from Barry Town, and so contented itself on that date with beginning a service of local passenger trains between Barry Dock and Cogan. A piquant feature of the inaugural ceremony was that the Cardiff contingent of guests travelled in a Taff Vale ordinary train to Penarth Dock station, and then walked the few yards to the Barry train waiting in Cogan station; history is silent as to whether the Barry management had to buy tickets for its guests over the T.V.R. section of the journey from Cardiff!

Thus the first section of the Barry Railway to be brought into use was one authorised later than those sanctioned by the Act of Incorporation. The Cogan branch is practically level throughout, with no engineering feature of note except a tunnel 222 yd. long, west of Cogan. The only intermediate station has always been Dinas Powis, which the Company's printer on occasion spelled Dynas Powis.

Meanwhile, the construction, equipment, and staffing of the dock and main railway, which had been going on apace, gathered final momentum as the opening of the dock approached. The first Barry engine had worked an inspection saloon over the full length of the main line from Hafod to Barry on 22 November 1888; the Barry Dock–Cogan passenger service was extended 1 m. 7 ch. westward to Barry station on 8 February 1889; and goods and mineral traffic began to be carried between Barry and Cogan, and between Cadoxton, Tynycaeau and the junction with the G.W.R. at St. Fagan's, all on 13 May 1889. Six weeks later, on 29 June, water was let into the dock, and on 18 July all was ready for

B

the ceremonial opening.   This was also the date on which
the conveyance of coal via the Hafod and Treforest junctions
officially began, though it must have begun very early in the
morning for six ships to be loading in the early afternoon!
The majority of the 2,000 invited guests travelled from
Cardiff in two special trains of new Barry coaches; this time
the management was risking no nonsense with the Taff Vale
at Cogan, and the trains were routed over the Great
Western's South Wales main line as far as St. Fagan's, thence
up the bank to Tynycaeau, and so by reversal down to
Cadoxton and Barry Dock, where a temporary platform had
been put up for the occasion.   Before noon the ceremonial
ribbon had been cut, the inaugural vessel had entered the
dock, and the first truckload of coal to be shipped at Barry
had roared down its tip into the waiting hold.

Immediate Success

This was David Davies's day.   In the absence of Lord
Windsor through a bereavement, he presided at the opening
ceremony, and though destined to live but another year and
two days, he saw the fulfilment of his dream.   One month
after the opening of Barry Dock, 8,200 tons of coal were
shipped in a single day from eight tips, and in the five
months for which it was open in 1889 the port dealt with
598 ships (461 steam and 137 sail) and exported just over
1 million tons of coal and coke.   In the first full year of
operation, 1890, the totals were to rise to 1,753 ships and
over 3 million tons of coal.   A dividend of 5 per cent was
declared for the second half-year of 1889, and one of 10 per
cent. for 1890.   By then David Davies had passed on;
Crawshay Bailey had died three years previously, and with
them went the last links between the primitive, pioneering
days of Welsh railways and the modern world which the
opening of the Barry Dock & Railways exemplified.   It was
a world which men like these had made possible.
Reaction of the opening of Barry both by and upon the
Taff Vale was instantaneous.   Helped by a subsidy from the
Marquis of Bute as an incentive to retain coal shipments
through Cardiff, the Taff Vale reduced its rate for shipment

coal, thus compelling the Barry in turn to drop its own rate below the level which it had planned. Through a combination of the reduction in rate and loss of traffic to the Barry, the Taff Vale gross revenue for 1890 fell by more than £170,000 below the 1888 figure. The Taff was hard hit for some years but, with the continuing expansion of the coalfield, it gradually recovered its prosperity.

The rates war between the two rivals was to drag on for some years. The famous Section 23 of the Barry Act of 1888, while requiring the Taff Vale to carry traffic to or from the Barry system at the lowest mileage rate at which the Taff carried like traffic to or from the docks at Cardiff, Penarth, or Barry, also provided for arbitration as to what bonus, if any, was to be allowed the Taff in respect of traffic exchanged at Hafod, which was clearly the most unfavourable exchange point so far as the Taff was concerned. In 1890 the Taff applied to the Railway & Canal Commission for a bonus of $2\frac{1}{2}$d. a ton on the Hafod exchange traffic. After long arguments the Commission granted a bonus of .2d. a ton, in respect only of traffic which originated more than four miles from Hafod, "and ordered the Taff Company to pay half the Barry Company's costs, as a very large part of the Enquiry had been taken up in exposing the fallacies and inaccuracies . . . put forward by the Taff Vale Company ".* By the Barry Act of 1894, it was enacted that the obligations imposed on the T.V.R. under Section 23 of the Barry Act of 1888 were to be deemed to be obligations for the benefit of the public as well as of the (Barry) Company, while by the Taff Vale's Act of 1896, Penarth Dock was determined as the standard point for determining the mileage rate for Barry traffic passing over the T.V.R.

Meanwhile the Barry dragon was rapidly spreading its wings. Even before the new dock had blossomed into activity, the company had been putting into shape its plans to extend eastward and north-eastward, so as to establish effective communication with Cardiff and to tap parts of the coalfield other than those served by the Taff Vale. There had been a false start in 1888, when a proposal for a line from the Barry system near St. Fagan's to a point about a

* *History of the Barry Railway Company.*

mile north of Llanishen station on the Rhymney Railway
north of Cardiff had been rejected by the House of Lords
Committee. Better fortune attended the promotion in the
following year of a Bill for a direct line from Cogan to
Cardiff, and for a connection to the Rhymney Railway and
the Aber Valley above Caerphilly. Although the Bill was
withdrawn, this was in consideration of mutual concessions
between the Barry and the Taff Vale, which were embodied
in an agreement dated 19 March 1890 and subsequently
confirmed by the Barry's Act of 5 August 1891. The Taff
Vale granted the Barry running powers for mineral and
goods traffic from Cogan to Walnut Tree Junction, Taffs
Well, where such traffic could be exchanged with the
Rhymney Railway; and for goods, mineral, and passenger
traffic from Cogan to Penarth Curve South Junction with
the G.W.R. From this point into Cardiff, both the Barry
and the Taff Vale looked for running powers over the Great
Western's Riverside Branch, opened for goods traffic in 1884,
which extended for nearly a mile from the south side of
Cardiff General station into the industrial area lying between
the River Taff and the Glamorganshire Canal. The Act
required the G.W.R. to convert the Riverside Branch for
passenger traffic within two years, failing which the Barry
would be entitled to make its own connecting line across the
Taff to join the Riverside Branch, to convert the latter into a
passenger line, and to build its own terminal station near the
Exchange, Mount Stuart Square, close to where Clarence
Road station now stands. In the event, the G.W.R. duly
converted the Riverside Branch and afforded the use of it to
both the Barry and the Taff Vale Railways.

Into Cardiff

The forging of the direct links with the Rhymney Railway and with Cardiff was of immense importance to the
Barry, not merely because of the additional sources of freight
traffic which were opened up, but also because the residential,
business, and workmen's passenger traffic was growing
rapidly. Although only 5 miles of line were open to
passenger traffic, the Barry Railway carried over $1\frac{1}{2}$ million

passengers during 1890, the service having already expanded to fifteen trains each way on weekdays, and the Taff Vale having previously conceded through booking facilities to and from the Barry system in order to avoid complaints of delay and congestion at Penarth.

It was not until 14 August 1893 that Barry trains began to run through to and from the Riverside platforms at Cardiff, but despite the traditional " gay decoration " of the first trains, the inaugural day of the new service was marred by the partial derailment of the 9.18 a.m. train from Cardiff to Barry, while passing over the curve off the T.V.R. at Cogan Junction. Fortunately, there were no serious personal injuries nor much damage to the new six-wheeled coaches, and the line was reopened by mid-day.*

The service was extended over the Riverside Branch to Clarence Road on 2 April 1894, the total service between Barry and Cardiff being seventeen trains each way on week-days, and the 9 miles taking about 28 minutes.

The years 1893–4 were also important for further expansion in and around Barry itself. By 1892 the coal and coke exports through the port had already topped 4 million tons a year, while the number of ships arriving exceeded 2,000 annually. The company was assuming growing responsibility as a port authority; under its Act of 1889 there had been established a Barry Pilotage Board independent of the Bristol Channel Pilotage, while the Barry's statutory powers embraced such varied matters as suppression of drunkenness by regulating the introduction of liquor into the docks for supply to ships, and the raising, removal or blowing up of wrecks. The need to extend the docks themselves had become quickly urgent after the opening of the port, and by its Act of 1893 the company was empowered to construct No. 2 Dock, 34 acres in extent, opening out of No. 1 Dock on the latter's east side. The new dock was opened in 1898, being equipped with coal tips on its north side and facilities for general cargo on the south side.

The Act of 1893 which authorised No. 2 Dock and its

* *The Western Mail*, 15 August 1893. There is no specific reference to this accident in the Board of Trade Accident Reports, 1893, but it may be inferred from the statistical tables that it was due to a broken carriage spring or axle.

connecting railways also contained the first provisions for rail communication with Barry Island, which with the advent of the railway to Barry was rapidly becoming a rival to Penarth as a seaside resort. By this Act the Barry Railway was empowered to build two tramroads totalling 1½ miles in length, mostly on reserved track; the whole concept suggested that a delegation of Barry officials had spent an enjoyable day on the Swansea & Mumbles. The main tramroad was to run from the road outside Barry station, across the artificial causeway which had been formed by the enclosure of part of the old harbour, to a terminus in Paget Road near the beach on Whitmore Bay; a short branch was to run from the junction of Paget Road and Plymouth Road to a terminus at Hewell Road. The tramroads were to be of 3 ft. 6 in. gauge and were to be worked by animal power, or, subject to Board of Trade approval, by steam power or any mechanical power; but specifically not by electrical power. The last-named reservation was most curious in view of the fact that the Barry Company had ample electrical power available to the nearby docks; it may have been either a politic concession to a directorate largely representative of coal interests, or perchance one in the eye for the Taff Vale, which was known to be toying with the future possibilities of electrification.

Barry Island never got its " Swansea & Mumbles ", however, for the tramroad idea was quietly dropped in favour of an orthodox railway extension from Barry to Barry Island, authorised the following year and opened on 3 August 1896. This branch, which was to help attract many thousands of holiday visitors to " the Island "—by now it was an island only in name—curved very sharply away from the west end of Barry station, descended the causeway on a ruling gradient of 1 in 80 (known as " Harbour Bank "), and rose at the same inclination to Barry Island station. Its original length was slightly less than ¾-mile; its subsequent extension to Barry Pier belongs to a later chapter.

While these extensions were taking place in the immediate vicinity of Barry itself, the company was seeking further expansion along its main line to the Rhondda. In 1893-5 the Barry had supported, if not inspired, the promotion of

the East Glamorgan Railway Company, which was intended
to link the Barry main line near Pontypridd with the
Rhymney and the Brecon & Merthyr Railways in the
vicinity of Bargoed, with a branch to Ynysybwl—a Taff
Vale preserve. Parliament would have none of the East
Glamorgan, nor was the Barry successful in its efforts to
extend further westward into the Rhondda Valley beyond
Hafod. Nevertheless, the Rhondda local authorities were
anxious to see direct communication for passenger traffic
established between the Rhondda Valley and the Barry
district, and during the proceedings in the 1894 Session on
the Barry's Bill for a line from Hafod to New Cymmer
Colliery, Porth, the chairman of the House of Lords Select
Committee, Lord Balfour of Burleigh, suggested that the
Taff Vale should give the Barry running powers for passenger
traffic into Porth, where connections could be made with the
Taff Vale trains serving both the *Rhondda Fawr* and the
Rhondda Fach. This being a small concession to make for
preventing the further extension of the Barry system into the
Rhondda, the Taff Vale accordingly made an agreement
which enabled the Barry Railway to begin passenger
service between Barry, Pontypridd, and Porth on 16 March
1896. The intermediate stations in their order from
Cadoxton were Wenvoe (2¾ miles), Creigiau (8¾ miles),
Efail Isaf (11 miles), Treforest (13 miles, added 1 April
1898), and Pontypridd (15 miles), the overall distance from
Barry to Porth being 20 miles. In order to minimise con-
fliction between the new passenger service and the frequent
freight trains, running loops or platform loops were provided
at most of the intermediate stations.

More Trouble with the Taff

The introduction of passenger service over the main line
encouraged the Barry to provide a direct service between
Pontypridd and Cardiff (Clarence Road), running over the
G.W.R. main line between St. Fagan's and Cardiff. This
began on 7 June 1897, but the agreement with the Taff Vale
did not extend to the Cardiff trains, which accordingly did
not run north of Pontypridd (B.R.) or " Graig " station, as it

was sometimes called. By this time, the growth in the volume of Barry Railway traffic using the T.V.R. between Cogan and Penarth Curve South Junction, together with the high tolls charged by the Taff Vale, had caused renewed friction between the two companies, which the inauguration of the Barry's Cardiff–Pontypridd service did nothing to mitigate. In 1897–8 the Barry therefore revived its project for an independent line into Cardiff, with a terminus at Mount Stuart Square, but withdrew the proposal upon its neighbour agreeing to modify the tolls and to provide additional tracks between Cogan and Penarth Curve South Junction. As an indication of the extent to which the Barry went in order to avoid paying mileage charges to the Taff Vale, merchandise and livestock traffic for exchange with the G.W.R. was worked as far as possible via St. Fagan's, where a tranship shed was built close to the junction with the G.W.R. main line.

The Western Flank

Also brought into use at this period was the Vale of Glamorgan Railway, which, although incorporated as a separate company that retained its nominal independence until 1922, was equipped and worked by the Barry, and to all intents and purposes formed part of the latter's system. The Vale of Glamorgan Railway had its genesis in the desire of the coalowners of the Llynvi, Garw, and Ogmore Valleys north of Bridgend for a better outlet for their shipment coal than was afforded by the limited facilities of Porthcawl, their nearest port, or by the combined G.W.R.–Barry Railway route to Barry via Tondu, Peterston, and Drope. They therefore promoted their own railway from Tondu along the southern coastal edge of the Vale to join the Barry Railway west of the port. Always eager to demand running powers over anybody and everybody else's railways, the Barry Company was less enthusiastic about admitting a third party into its own domain. Being sensitive, however, both as to its exposed flank to the west, and to the threat of the Taff Vale Railway to move down into the Vale by an extension from Cowbridge to the small and ancient port of

Aberthaw, the Barry came to terms with the V. of G. promoters. The Act of 26 August 1889 which incorporated the
Vale of Glamorgan Railway Company, with a capital of
£360,000, accordingly also confirmed an agreement made
with the Barry company to work the railway when opened
for 60 per cent. of the gross receipts. Despite this additional
support the new company had difficulty in raising its capital,
which was not forthcoming until the Barry company, under
powers conferred by its Act of 1893, undertook to guarantee
the V. of G. shareholders a 4 per cent. dividend out of the
Barry's own share of the gross receipts. In return, the Barry
company obtained the right to nominate four directors of
the V. of G., which thereafter became almost entirely a Barry
subsidiary, although a later attempt in 1902–3 to amalgamate the two companies was unsuccessful.

Owing to its having to be constructed through limestone
country, the Vale of Glamorgan Railway, for which Sir
James Szlumper was engineer, proved both tedious and
costly to build. From its starting-point at Coity Junction
with the G.W.R. between Bridgend and Tondu, the line
passed round the back of Bridgend through the first of
several limestone cuttings, crossed over the G.W.R. main
line east of Bridgend station, and at Cowbridge Road
Junction (1¾ miles) threw off a north-westerly spur, 33 ch.
in length, to join the Great Western immediately on the
Cardiff side of Bridgend station, into which the Barry
Railway exercised running powers on behalf of the Vale of
Glamorgan. Continuing towards Barry, the Vale line
climbed out of the Ogmore River vale on ruling gradients of
1 in 173 and 1 in 141, but steeper gradients were met with
further east, including the River Thaw bank at 1 in 85 and
1 in 82 down towards Aberthaw, and 1 in 87 falling through
Porthkerry cutting. The heaviest engineering work was
reserved for the last section, where the line traversed Porthkerry Park by means of two short tunnels (Porthkerry No. 1,
545 yd., and Porthkerry No. 2, 71 yd.), a substantial embankment, and the Porthkerry viaduct, before an end-on junction
with the Barry proper, just west of Barry station.

The Vale of Glamorgan Railway, comprising 20¾ miles
of double line, with platform loops at Southerndown Road,

Llantwit Major, and Aberthaw, was opened for traffic on 1 December 1897, and was almost immediately closed again through the subsidence of a pier of Porthkerry viaduct and part of the embankment in the early hours of 10 January 1898. This masonry structure, 110 ft. above ground level at its highest point, consists of thirteen arched spans of 50 ft. and three of 45 ft.; its construction was begun in 1894 and completed in July 1897, having given a good deal of trouble owing to failure of the foundations. While the viaduct was being repaired and strengthened, the Vale of Glamorgan Railway was closed between Barry and Rhoose until 25 April 1898, when a temporary diversion line 2 m. 44 ch. in length was opened round the north side of the crippled structure, being used for passenger as well as goods trains. In the intervening three months between the closure of the railway and the opening of the diversion, passengers were carried between Barry and Rhoose in a horse-drawn brake. This loop line was built without Parliamentary powers, retrospective authority being conferred by the Vale of Glamorgan's Act of 6 June 1899. The viaduct was reopened for goods traffic on 8 January 1900, and for passenger trains on 9 April.

A Springboard for Aggression

Owing to its relatively high cost of operation over the heavy gradients, and to the failure of the shipment coal traffic to expand on the scale expected because of the development of Port Talbot nearer to the Ogmore coalfield, the Vale of Glamorgan Railway never became a very lucrative investment for the Barry company. Moreover, local originating traffic was very meagre: the only industry on the line comprised the lime and cement works at Rhoose and Aberthaw, and quarries towards the western end. But its acquisition secured the approaches to Barry from the west, and it afforded a potential jumping-off point for several ventures which, if successful, would have carried the Barry's banner nearly to Swansea.

In 1895, the Vale of Glamorgan figured in the grandiose project for a London & South Wales Railway, the promoters of which included prominent men associated with the Barry company, whose engineers were also named in the proposal. It was intended that the new company should have running powers over the Barry Railway and the Vale of Glamorgan, the latter promoting its own Bill for a branch from Ewenny to the Rhondda & Swansea Bay Railway at Port Talbot. Beyond reasonable doubt, the real object of the London & South Wales promoters was to force the Great Western to carry out its South Wales Direct line, and to make certain concessions to the South Wales coal trade. In this they succeeded, and the London & South Wales scheme was withdrawn in 1896.* In later years, however, the Barry directors continued to toy with the idea of westward extensions; as late as 1908, the company obtained powers to subscribe to the proposed Neath, Pontardawe & Brynamman Railway, which had been moribund since obtaining its Act of Incorporation in 1895. The Barry, the Midland, the Rhondda & Swansea Bay, and the Port Talbot Railways were all empowered to enter into working agreements with the Neath, Pontardawe & Brynamman, but the Great Western concluded agreements with the R.S.B. and the Port Talbot Railways whereby those companies were virtually taken over, thus effectually excluding the Barry from west of Bridgend.

The last section of the Barry Railway proper to be opened before the end of the century was the Pier Branch which had been authorised in 1896 and was brought into use on 27 June 1899. It comprises an end-on extension, half a mile in length, of the Barry Island Branch, descending at 1 in 80 through a tunnel 280 yd. long, and terminating alongside the Low Water Landing Pontoon, close to and on the west side of the main entrance lock into Barry Docks. The Pier station originally comprised two long platforms, with two middle roads for stabling and shunting. The Landing Pontoon for pleasure steamers is sheltered by the Western Breakwater, on which runs a dock tramroad that passes behind the west side of No. 1 Dock and cuts through

---

* See B. G. Wilson, " The London & South Wales Railway ", *Railway Magazine*, October 1956.

the cliff by a tunnel, unfaced except by the native rock; the
exit portals of the two tunnels are close to and at right angles
to one another at the Barry end of the Pier station, and the
tramroad alignment finally crosses the Pier Branch on the
level, a movable track being laid down when it is required
to work to the breakwater. Another curious feature of the
Island & Pier Branch is that the degree of curvature is so
great after leaving the main line at Barry that a train to the
Pier completely reverses its direction in little over a mile,
while a train from Cardiff (Clarence Road) to the Pier
starts facing almost due North, turns round to the South-
West, and finishes up facing due East.

Steamers in the Bristol Channel

The Pier Branch was never used by regular public
services in the ordinary sense, being provided solely for the
summer cruises by Bristol Channel pleasure steamers. Prior
to the branch being brought into use, the Barry company
had applied for Parliamentary powers to run steamboats
between Barry, Weston-super-Mare, and other resorts, but
was defeated by the opposition of other railway companies
and of the established steamboat operators, principally
P. & A. Campbell. The latter's boats began calling at
Barry Pier in July 1899, and more than 49,000 steamer
passengers travelled to and from the pier by rail during that
season. In the following year, the calls at Barry Pier were
suspended in default of agreement as to the guarantee
required by Campbell's. The service was resumed in
1901–2, but so far from railway passengers gaining by the
quicker rail trip from Cardiff to join the steamers, the latter
often arrived full up, so that Barry passengers had to stand,
or were left behind.

Accordingly the Barry company renewed its application
for Parliamentary powers to run its own steamers. These
powers were duly granted by the Barry Railway (Steam
Vessels) Act of 15 August 1904, but were so hedged about
with restrictions framed to prevent the B.R. from engaging
in the coastal cargo trade, and to protect the existing
pleasure-cruise operators, that the prospects of commercial

success were dubious from the outset. Thus, the Barry steamers were permitted to carry only " passengers and their luggage, perishable merchandise and also such small consignments of other merchandise as are usually carried by steam vessels constructed for and engaged in such passenger traffic ", and then only between Barry and places on the south side of the Bristol Channel between Weston-super-Mare and Ilfracombe, both inclusive. For summer excursion traffic they were allowed to ply as far westward as Tenby or Hartland Point, and into Bristol or Clevedon, but voyages had always to start from or terminate at Barry, while passengers could not be re-embarked at Bristol or Clevedon unless they had been brought over from Barry!

The Barry Railway fleet began operations in 1905 with two paddle-steamers, *Gwalia* and *Devonia*, built new by John Brown's, and a third, *Westonia*, which had been built by Scott's of Kinghorn in 1899, and which had several previous owners. The P.S. *Barry* was added from Brown's in 1907, in which year over 191,000 railway passengers travelled via Barry Pier. In an attempt to get round the statutory inhibitions, the ships had meanwhile been transferred to a separate company known as The Barry & Bristol Channel Steamship Company (" the Red Funnel Line "), but this led to litigation and to the termination of the separate ownership. In other attempts to widen the scope of operations, the Barry Company in 1907 became a party to the Burnham (Somerset) Pier Company, which by its Act of 26 July 1907 was incorporated to acquire the pier at Burnham-on-Sea, already closely associated with the Somerset & Dorset Railway—the last-named concern had operated shipping services in the Bristol Channel for many years. One of the objects of the Act of 1907 was " to facilitate the transmission of steamer traffic to and from Barry ", and the B.R. Company was empowered to subscribe up to £15,000. In the following year the Barry sought Parliamentary powers to subscribe to the companies owning the two piers at Weston, and to make working agreements with the owners and managers of the piers at Weston, Minehead, and Ilfracombe. As late as February 1909 the Barry Company's chairman told the shareholders—a section

of whom was urging that the company should cut its losses
on the steamers—that the directors "had no hesitation in
deciding that the passenger steamship services should be
continued ". But exactly a year later he announced that
negotiations were in progress for the sale of the steamers,
and by August 1910 all four had been disposed of; they had
cost £104,470, and the net loss on realisation was £36,000.
Their varied and gallant record of service afterwards is no
part of this story but, after their departure from Barry Pier,
Campbell's White Funnel Steamers resumed calling there,
and do so to this day.

Apart from the pleasure steamers, the Barry company in
its capacity as a dock authority owned and operated various
tugs, dredgers and other harbour craft, including a floating
fire-engine.

The last five years of the nineteenth century represented
a period of notable expansion by the Barry Railway, in the
course of which it had opened its second dock, secured its
exposed western flank in the Vale of Glamorgan, and
greatly extended its passenger services. In 1898, towards
the end of which year the new dock was opened, coal and
coke exports were heavily hit by a coal strike, but in the
following year they rose to more than 7 million tons, and two
years later were to exceed the total shipped at Cardiff, so
making Barry the greatest coal-shipping port in the country.
In 1899, the number of ships using the port exceeded 3,000
for the first time.

Driving to the North-East

This same period witnessed also the start of the Barry's
culminating campaign to reach major new sources of traffic,
and to penetrate by stages to the Rhymney Valley, to the
Brecon & Merthyr Railway, and to the West Monmouthshire coalfield. Of these three stages, the first two were
accomplished by 1905, but the third was destined never to be
achieved. Many hard words were to be said in and out of
Parliament about the Barry's drive north-eastward across the
Taff and Rhymney Rivers into Monmouthshire, and it is
only fair to record that to the coalowners the Barry was rarely

an unwelcome entrant, while the shippers and agents were equally anxious to see the shortest and quickest routes opened up to the most modern of South Wales ports, with direct access to deep water.

Since 1891 the Barry had enjoyed access to the Rhymney Railway at Walnut Tree Junction by running powers over the T.V.R. via Cogan and Radyr, but the exchange across the Taff Vale main line at Walnut Tree was awkward and slow, and clearly would soon be incapable of coping with the rate of increase in traffic. Moreover, the Barry sought both a shorter route down from the Rhymney which would enable effective competitive rates to be quoted for traffic to Barry, and a deeper penetration into the preserves of the Taff Vale and Rhymney Railways. It was also hoped by connection with the Rhymney Railway's big neighbour, the London & North Western, not only to attract traffic from the Sirhowy Valley and from the Merthyr, Tredegar & Abergavenny line of the L.N.W.R., but also to give express goods service for general cargo traffic between Barry and the Midlands and North of England.

The Barry's Parliamentary proposals for the 1896 Session therefore included not only a direct line from Tynycaeau across country to the Rhymney Railway near Caerphilly, but also running powers over the whole of the R.R. system north of the new junction, and over the Taff Bargoed Joint Line of the Great Western and Rhymney Railways up to the Dowlais industrial district. The offensive was not launched a moment too soon, because the Bute Docks Company was belatedly moving to gain some measure of control over the railways bringing coal into Cardiff, by seeking to absorb the Glamorganshire Canal and the Rhymney Railway and so creating a railway system of its own, with extensive running powers. In the event, the Bute–Rhymney amalgamation project failed, while the Barry by its Act of 7 August 1896 was empowered to make its new line, nearly 7 miles long, from Tynycaeau to Penrhos (Upper) Junction with the Rhymney Railway at a point where the latter's branch from Walnut Tree was joined by the Pontypridd, Caerphilly & Newport Railway, about a mile west of Caerphilly. The Barry was also authorised to make a second line, slightly

over 2 miles long, leaving its own new route at Penrhos
(Lower) Junction, 50 ch. below the Upper Junction, climb-
ing to cross over the Barry, Rhymney, and P.C. & N. lines
at the Upper Junction, and terminating by a junction with
the Aber Valley (Senghenydd) Branch of the R.R., between
Penyrheol and Abertridwr stations. (The powers for this
latter branch were kept alive for some years but eventually
lapsed, it being found quite easy to work coal traffic from
the Aber Branch for Barry over other local junctions.) All
the running powers which the Barry had asked for were
refused by Parliament, save that the Barry Company was
awarded running powers into Caerphilly station for passenger
traffic, such powers only to be exercised compulsorily if the
Board of Trade should decide, at the application of the
Glamorganshire County Council, that the powers should be
so exercised. No regular use of these running powers was in
fact ever made, because the Rhymney Company claimed
that its Caerphilly station was so busy that it would have to
be enlarged at the Barry's expense to accommodate the
latter's trains, and the Barry " was not having any ". It was
not until 13 July 1907, when King Edward VII visited
Caerphilly, that the B.R. first ran excursions into the
Rhymney stronghold.

Over the Nantgarw Gap

Although barely 7 miles long, the Barry's new line from
Tynycaeau to Penrhos was not opened for mineral traffic
until 1 August 1901. This was due to the heavy engineering
work involved in bridging the Nantgarw Gap at Taffs Well,
a great natural fault in the rock barrier marking the southern
limit of the Glamorgan coalfield. For more than a century
before the Barry Railway came, the mineral wealth of
Glamorgan had flowed through this defile to the sea, and
through or into it there passed two roads, the River Taff, the
Glamorganshire Canal, an industrial tramroad, and the
Taff Vale, the Rhymney, and later the Cardiff Railways.
The Barry made no attempt to squeeze its way through the
pass, but, sweeping down from Penrhos Junction at a maximum falling gradient of 1 in 81, took straight off from the

50. *Seal of the Barry Railway Company*

51. *The Railway's Armorial Device*

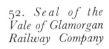

52. *Seal of the Vale of Glamorgan Railway Company*

53. *B.R. train for Barry (left) at Bridgend station about the turn of the century, with G.W.R. up main line express at centre*

54. *Llanbradach Viaduct, looking over the Rhymney Railway (in foreground) across the valley to the Brecon & Merthyr Railway*

55. *Signals at west end of Barry station about 1897, showing Vale of Glamorgan Railway (right) and line to Barry Island (left)*

56. *Barry Docks, looking west across no. 2 Dock to no. 1 Dock and Barry Island (top centre)*

57. *Walnut Tree Viaduct, seen from the former Taff Vale Railway line below, looking north.*

58. *2–4–2T no. 97 Barry Railway train approaching Riverside station, Cardiff*

59. *Train for Bridgend leaving Barry in Barry Railway period*

60. *Pontypridd station, looking towards north end of Treforest tunnel*

61. *The first design of Barry locomotives: no. 5 of class A* (1888)

62. *0–6–2 T no. 77 of class B1, built* 1894

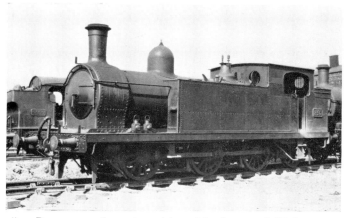

63. *Barry no. 54 in service, with modifications, as G.W.R. no.* 245

64. 0–6–0 *saddle tank no.* 47, *class F* (1890)

65. *A group of Barry Railway worthies posed round* 0–8–0 *no.* 35, *with tender-cab.*

66. 2–4–2 *T no.* 86 (*Hudswell, Clarke,* 1897) *at Barry station*

67. *No. 22 as originally built as* 2–4–0 *T*

68. 0–4–4 *T no.* 66 *of class G* (*Vulcan Foundry*, 1892)

69. 2–4–2 *T no.* 90 *of class J* (1898)

70. *The American-built 0–6–2 T, no. 119 of 1899, as rebuilt by Barry Railway with B1 boiler.*

71. *" Yankee " no. 118 rebuilt by G.W.R. and running as their no. 194*

72. *A rare photograph of the last Barry locomotive, 0–6–4 T no. 148, running as G.W.R. no. 1357, rebuilt with G.W.R. boiler*

73. *Barry Railway no. 79, the first British 0–8–2 T (Sharp, Stewart, 1896)*

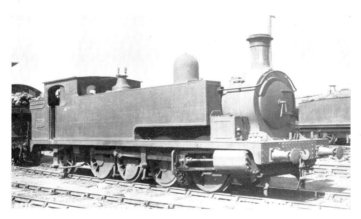

74. *Barry 0–8–2 T no. 83, running as G.W.R. no. 1384*

75. *0–6–4 T no. 143, of class L, as originally built, 1914*

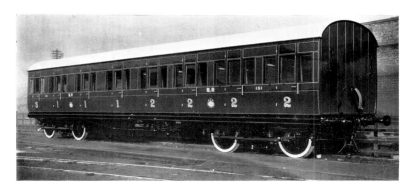

76. *Tri-composite Carriage no. 151, built 1920*

77. *Down Advance Starting signal at Southerndown Road, May 1961, showing last design of Barry Railway pressed-metal arm, with double white stripes*

78. *Steam railcar no. 2 (North British Locomotive Co., 1905)*

79. 0–6–0 T *no. 33, temporarily converted to* 0–4–2 T *for working improvised " auto-train ", with close-coupled 4-wheeled and 6-wheeled coaches*

80. *The last locomotive built for the Barry Railway,* 0–6–4 T *no. 148, posed for an official photograph on a 7-coach bogie suburban set*

hillside across the Gap to soar 120 ft. above its predecessors on the magnificent Walnut Tree viaduct, comprising seven steel lattice girder spans resting on massive masonry piers, and having a total length of 1,548 ft. At its western end the viaduct is slightly curved to enable the line to bend on to a shelf on the hillside, whence it runs through the Garth Woods and tunnel (490 yd.) on towards Tynycaeau, partly rising at 1 in 108 against the loaded coal trains. Within three years of its opening, the new line would be carrying 1½ million tons of Rhymney coal a year to Barry, but the Barry did not wait the completion of the Rhymney Branch before pressing on to its next objective. If it could not get up into the Rhymney Valley by running powers over the Rhymney Railway, it would get there another way: by crossing the valley to join the Brecon & Merthyr Railway on the far side. The impoverished B. & M. exacted a good price (including the payment by the Barry of the cost of doubling much of the B. & M. line) for the running powers which it granted up to Rhymney (B. & M.) for coal, coke, and pitwood traffic.

So by its Act of 1898 the Barry Railway got powers to extend from its projected Aber Branch of 1896, over the bottom end of the Aber Valley and the R.R. Senghenydd Branch by a long viaduct, and then by an even longer viaduct over both the Rhymney's main line at Energlyn and the full width of the Rhymney Valley to join the B. & M. near Duffryn Isaf, 1½ miles north of Bedwas station, the actual point of junction being known as Barry Junction (B. & M.). Including the initial length of the previously-authorised Aber Branch which was absorbed in the new B. & M. Extension, the total length from Penrhos Lower Junction to Barry Junction (B. & M.) was nearly 3¾ miles, and there was in addition a half-mile connection off the new line at Energlyn North Junction down to the Rhymney at Energlyn South Junction. The summit level of the Barry Railway, 382 ft. above sea level, was found near Energlyn North Junction.

The B. & M. Extension was not heavily graded, the ruling inclinations being 1 in 175 falling from the Aber (Penyrheol) viaduct towards Penrhos Junction, and 1 in 104

c

falling between the two Energlyn Junctions. But it was a very expensive railway; whereas the Rhymney Branch had cost £270,000, the B. & M. Extension cost £500,000, of which about half was represented by the latter's engineering *pièce-de-résistance*, the Llanbradach viaduct.* Ranking among the greatest of South Wales bridges, this tremendous structure, 2,400 ft. long with eleven lattice steel girders resting on brick piers, towered 125 ft. above the valley floor as it carried the Barry lines with splendid arrogance across the Rhymney River and so on to (technically) English soil, for the east side of the river lies in Monmouthshire.

It was not until 2 January 1905 that the B. & M. Extension was opened for coal traffic. It was never used for regular passenger services, but on 24 April 1905 the first of many excursion trains passed over it *en route* to Barry. The completion of the link with the Brecon & Merthyr Railway marked, in effect, the completion also of the main system of the Barry Railway, but the men behind it did not think so at the time, nor in the current flush of success could they visualise that all that lay beyond the mountain-face at Duffryn Isaf was a decade of Parliamentary struggle and ultimate frustration.

The Last Offensive

The hammers were still ringing out along Llanbradach viaduct when the Barry launched its last offensive into the mountains: a two-pronged drive of which the left prong was to be thrust up past Bargoed towards Dowlais, and the right prong was directed upon the rich and fast-developing coal measures of the Sirhowy and the Monmouthshire Western Valleys.

Dealing first with the Bargoed project: the motive for this lay in the fact that the Barry's running powers over the B. & M. were useless in respect of the latter's route to Dowlais, since this could only be reached over the $2\frac{3}{4}$ miles of Rhymney metals which separated the Northern and Southern Sections of the B. & M. Between 1904 and 1907, therefore, the Barry made several attempts to outflank the

---

* Llanbradach, on the former R.R. main line, was the nearest station to the west end of the viaduct.

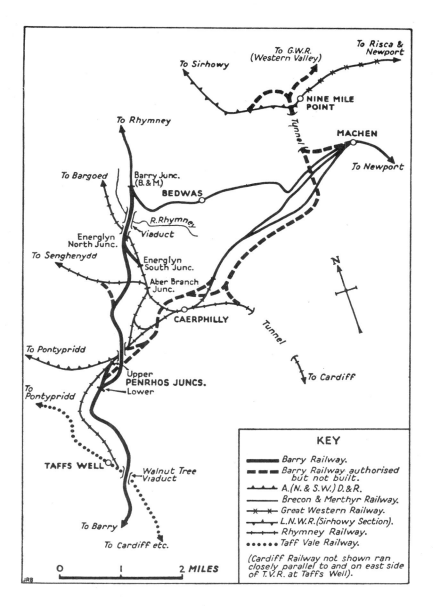

To Sirhowy

To G.W.R.
(Western Valley)

To Risca &
Newport

NINE MILE
POINT

Tunnel

MACHEN

To Rhymney

To Newport

To Bargoed

Barry Junc.
(B.& M.)

BEDWAS

R.Rhymney
Viaduct

Energlyn
North Junc.

To Senghenydd

Energlyn
South Junc.

Aber Branch
Junc.

CAERPHILLY

Tunnel

To Pontypridd

To Cardiff

Upper
PENRHOS JUNCS.
Lower

To
Pontypridd

N

TAFFS WELL

Walnut Tree
Viaduct

KEY

Barry Railway.

Barry Railway authorised
but not built.

A.(N.& S.W.) D.& R.

Brecon & Merthyr Railway.

Great Western Railway.

L.N.W.R.(Sirhowy Section).

Rhymney Railway.

Taff Vale Railway.

(Cardiff Railway not shown ran
closely parallel to and on east side
of T.V.R. at Taffs Well).

To Barry

To Cardiff etc.

0   1   2 MILES

JRB

183

Rhymney Railway in the Bargoed Rhymney Valley, by
promoting a line which would have left the B. & M. south of
Aberbargoed and would have rejoined it north of Deri
Junction. Even by South Wales standards, this would have
been a remarkable railway, involving heavy bridgework to
cross over both the B. & M. Rhymney Branch and the main
line of the R.R., a tunnel 220 yd. long through the ridge
between the main Rhymney Valley and that of the Bargoed
Rhymney, and a ruling gradient rising northward of 1 in 43,
with a good deal more at 1 in 48. Eventually in August 1908
it was announced that this scheme had been withdrawn on a
traffic agreement being reached with the Rhymney Company, thus finally dispelling an expectation confided by the
Barry chairman to the shareholders, that the Barry would
be able to enjoy running powers to Aberystwyth!

The Attack on Monmouthshire

The Barry's attempted invasion of the Monmouthshire
Valleys was a much bigger affair; indeed, although con-
centrated in less than 10 miles of ground, it probably
involved more protagonists, and cost more in Parliamentary
expenses (the Barry's alone were reputed to be £100,000),
than any other railway project since the Great Central came
to London a few years earlier. The proposal to cut through
the mountain barrier dividing the Rhymney and Sirhowy
Valleys, and so to open a new route for export coal instead
of going round by Newport, was by no means new: the
Brecon & Merthyr had sponsored such a project as early as
1865, while in 1888 the Rhymney Railway, with L.N.W.R.
support, had obtained powers for a line from Nine Mile
Point to Caerphilly. When the G.W.R. succeeded in buying
off the Rhymney Railway for a consideration of £10,000 a
year, the Bute Docks Company secured the transfer to itself
of the authority to build this Nine Mile Point–Caerphilly
line, and the Barry Railway in turn exacted contingent
running rights if the line were built; but the constructional
powers became time-expired without anything being done
to exercise them.

In 1904, the Barry launched out afresh with a proposal to cut through the mountain from near Barry Junction (B. & M.) to Ynysddu on the Sirhowy line of the L.N.W.R., with a branch up the Sirhowy Valley to join the G.W.R. Pontypool–Neath route at Penar Junction. This scheme drew down upon the Barry the wrath of no fewer than seven railway companies and of the Newport Corporation, Harbour Commissioners, and Chamber of Commerce. Even the Barry's ally the Brecon & Merthyr objected because none of the new traffic would pass over it, so when the Barry's scheme was revived in 1906 after an initial failure in the Session of 1905, the invader offered both to make a different form of junction at Duffryn Isaf whereby all the Barry's Sirhowy traffic would pass over 2 ch. of the B. & M., and to lease the whole B. & M. if powers could be obtained.

The conflicts which raged over these and subsequent schemes before successive Parliamentary Committees attracted a truly formidable array of expert witnesses and forensic talent. Among famous general managers who gave evidence were Inglis of the Great Western, Harrison of the North Western, and Robert Miller of the Caledonian, while the Grand Old Man of the Welsh railways, Cornelius Lundie of the Rhymney, appeared in the witness-box at 92 years of age. Distinguished counsel vied with one another in castigating the Barry as " sordid and greedy ", " the spoiled child of Parliament " (Mr. Pollock, K.C.), and as " a marauding company " (Mr. Balfour Browne, K.C., who added that it was " not a question of Heaven knowing where the Barry will stop; only the other place knows "). Nor was the liveliness confined to the committee rooms. A public meeting convened at Caerphilly to ventilate the merits of the rival projects broke up in disorder when stink-bombs were thrown in the hall, and was concluded by candle-light in the open air, with awkward questions as to which railway company had paid for hiring the hall.

The crucial Parliamentary Session was that of 1907. By this time the Barry had abandoned the idea of the Barry Junction–Ynysddu tunnel, and shifted its route eastward to run from Penrhos via Caerphilly and Machen, and thence by tunnel through Machen Mountain to Nine Mile Point.

Two other and largely parallel routes, which initially had
been promoted by the L.N.W.R. individually and by the
Great Western and Rhymney jointly, had now been consoli-
dated into a tripartite scheme, which at its bottom end
would have linked up with the main Rhymney line to
Cardiff, north of Caerphilly Tunnel. Realising the strong
support which the Barry commanded from the coal trade and
from the Cardiff Chamber of Commerce, the three partners
now offered the Barry traffic facilities over the proposed
tripartite line if the Barry would withdraw its Bill. The
Barry in turn offered to promote a fresh Bill acceptable to all
parties, including the Taff Vale and Cardiff Companies as
partners should they so wish. These consultations foundered
on the issue that always made the Barry " not just a horse of
a different colour, but a different animal " : as a dock owner,
the Barry was ready to divide the mileage receipts, but not
the terminal charges. So the rival schemes went ahead for
the bitterest fight of all, culminating in the defeat of the
joint scheme, and the approval of the Barry Bill, which
received the Royal Assent on 28 August 1907.

The Authorised Line

   The railways so authorised aggregated about 10 miles in
length, and extended from Penrhos Junction eastward,
passing to the north of Caerphilly, where a junction was to
be made with the Caerphilly Branch of the B. & M. Turning north near the Rhymney River it would pass in tunnel
through Machen Mountain to emerge between Nine Mile
Point and Ynysddu. Here it would have forked left to join
the L.N.W.R., and right to join the G.W.R. Western Valleys
lines near Cross Keys. A short branch would have led
from the south end of the Sirhowy Tunnel to join the
B. & M. near Machen station. The last-named spur formed
part of a comprehensive agreement with the B. & M.,
separately ratified by the Barry Act of 1909, whereby the
B. & M. would have had extensive running powers over the
Barry lines of 1907, while the Barry would have had running
powers to Bassaleg for passenger traffic, thus opening up
access to Newport for the Barry Railway.

But what appeared to be another resounding victory for the Barry Railway proved to be only a Pyrrhic one. The House of Lords Committee, in seeking to preserve the interests of the various railway companies and ports, had inserted a clause requiring the rates per ton per mile on the new railways to be the same, irrespective of whether the traffic was destined for Cardiff, Penarth, Barry, or Newport. As the distance from the Sirhowy Valley to Cardiff was 12 miles, compared with 18 miles to Barry, the Barry Company considered that the effect of this Section 23 in its Act of 1907 " would be to deprive them of the usual power to charge rates varying in proportion to the distance for which the traffic is conveyed ". Clearly the Barry feared that it would not be worth spending about £700,000 on the new lines if it were to be unable to undercut its neighbours enjoying traffic facilities over these lines on payment of mileage charges only. The Barry therefore did nothing to build the new lines (to the fury of the Brecon & Merthyr, which had withdrawn its own scheme for a line to the Sirhowy in consequence of its deal with the Barry), but returned to Parliament for the repeal or amendment of Section 23. Some amendment was granted under the Barry's Act of 1911, but it did not go far enough for the Barry, and after the constructional powers had been further renewed, the Great War came in 1914 to dispel for ever the vision of a breakthrough to the Monmouthshire coalfield. A minor consolation which the Barry derived from this long spell of Parliamentary warfare was the defeat of a proposal to amalgamate the Cardiff and the Rhymney Companies with the Taff Vale, which had it come to fruition would have placed the Barry in a very awkward position.

While those long-drawn struggles were in progress, the trade of Barry Docks continued to expand, and during the first decade of the new century the annual rate of dividend only once fell to as low as 6 per cent. But the directors were confronted with many anxieties, and some critical voices among the shareholders at the half-yearly meetings. The Rhymney and B. & M. Extension lines had been costly and rather slow in building; the Vale of Glamorgan represented a strategic rather than a financial gain; and the protracted Parliamentary proceedings had not only been very expensive, but also absorbed a high proportion of the officers' time. The extensions of the docks system and the provision of new rolling-stock added to the financial burden, while the incidence of heavy repairs to locomotives which had been hard-worked from the outset rose sharply during the early years of the century. (In 1904 a committee of directors with the general manager and engineer went to the Continent to study possible electrification, but returned with the conclusion " that under present conditions the application of electrical power to railways having heavy mineral traffic is impracticable ".) Other targets of shareholders' criticisms were the splendid new General Offices (fronted by a statue of David Davies) at Barry Dock, which were completed at the turn of the century and were reputed to have cost £50,000, and the sharp rise in the shunting mileage, which was primarily due to the growing practice in the coal trade of shipping mixed cargoes, calling for complex marshalling in the reception and sorting yard at Cadoxton. The steamboat service, and the investment ventures in Burnham Pier and the Neath, Pontardawe & Brynamman, also came under attack; but all these points of criticism were part of a general reaction to the dividend rate failing to keep pace with the growth of business.

Prosperity Regained

After several difficult meetings, the directors called in John Conacher, chairman and former general manager of the Cambrian Railways, initially as consultant, but as from 10 February 1910 he was appointed managing director. Conacher was not the first holder of this office with the Barry undertaking, Edward Davies (the son of " Dai Davies the Ocean ") having held it from 1890 to 1897. Although Conacher's régime was cut very short by his death in 1911, he introduced some austerities, and it was probably his influence that led the board to their sudden change of heart over the steamer service. At any rate, there were few grumbles from shareholders in subsequent years, for the ordinary dividend went back to 10 per cent. in 1912, and not less than 9½ per cent. was paid in any year thereafter, the return for the last three years of the company's life, 1919–21, being 10 per cent. annually.

In 1913, the last year before the First World War, coal and coke shipments from Barry Docks reached the record total of over 11 million tons. During this war, as later in the second, Barry played a worthy part in the movement of essential traffic, the peak year being 1916 when nearly 4,000 vessels of all kinds, aggregating over 5 million registered tons, were dealt with; the company moreover had released for service with the Forces nearly 800 of its staff, representing over 25 per cent. of the number employed.

Things were never the same again after the war. The world market for coal had been hard hit, shipping was progressively changing over to oil fuel, and the shadow of the Railways Act, 1921, now fell over the smaller railway companies. Along with some of its neighbours, the Barry stood out successfully to become a constituent rather than a subsidiary of the Western Group, becoming amalgamated with the G.W.R. on and from 1 January 1922. The financial terms reflected the strength of the Barry's position, each £100 of Barry Ordinary Stock being exchanged for £220 G.W.R. 5 per cent. Stock.

The last ordinary general meeting of the Barry Railway Company was held on 17 February 1922, but a special meeting was held later on 5 April formally to approve the terms of amalgamation. At both these meetings the Earl of Plymouth presided, having been chairman throughout the life of the company; he was nominated to become a director of the G.W.R. Another who had served throughout was G. C. Downing, the solicitor and sometime secretary. During its lifetime the company had four general managers: Richard Evans from the Rhymney Railway, who retired in 1905; Edward Lake from the North Eastern, retired 1912; T. H. Rendell from the G.W.R., retired 1919; and William Waddell. The last-named had taken part as a young man in the construction of the undertaking, and was the engineer from 1903 until 1919, when he became general manager. At the amalgamation he became docks assistant to the chief engineer, G.W.R.

In its final year (1921) of independent operation, the
Barry Railway carried 2¾ million passengers (excluding
" seasons ") originating on its system, and over 931,000 tons
of originating goods and mineral traffic, plus a vastly greater
coal traffic originating on other railways. Its engines ran an
aggregate mileage of nearly 2 million, the character of its
operations being mirrored by the proportions, within this
total, of some 708,000 freight engine-miles, and over 600,000
miles on freight shunting. Ultimate total capital expenditure
was £6,419,000, while for the final year gross receipts were
£1,733,000 and net receipts nearly £360,000. Few railways
accomplished so much in so small a compass; the total route
mileage, including the 20½ miles of the Vale of Glamorgan,
amounted to 67 m. 69 ch., and the aggregate track mileage,
including sidings, to some 300.

Traffic Working

The highly intensive and efficient traffic working of the
Barry Railway comprised the bulk movement of coal
between the valleys and the port reception sidings; the trip
working between the reception sidings and the coal hoists,
whereby a single ship could be coaled at 600 tons an hour;
some import and general merchandise traffic; and the
passenger services. The focal point of the coal movement
was Cadoxton Sidings, to which the bulk coal trains from
Trehafod or Treforest Junctions ran non-stop in about an
hour; the trains off the B. & M. took longer because they
picked up traffic at pits in the Rhymney Valley. In 1921,
there were about seventy-five booked and conditional coal
trains from these starting-points each weekday, together with
about a dozen booked trains from Peterston to Cadoxton via
Drope. At this time, there were also nine booked trains a
day of Monmouthshire coal from Rogerstone Yard (G.W.R.)
to Barry. Even before the First World War, the Monmouthshire traffic had become so heavy that the G.W.R. had
obtained Parliamentary powers to build a flyover at Ebbw
Junction, west of Newport, which would have carried the
Barry traffic over the G.W. main line to join the goods lines
on the south side, while during the 1914–18 period, and

afterwards until grouping, Barry Railway engines handled some of the trains between Rogerstone and Barry.

There being no direct run from the Cogan direction into Cadoxton Sidings, the Monmouthshire coal trains, also the exchange trip trains from Penarth Curve South Junction (T.V.R.), terminated at the Dock Sidings which extend almost the whole way from Cadoxton to Barry Docks station, and from which a burrowing junction was constructed in 1898–9 to give direct access to the coal tips on No. 1 Dock. This great array of sidings at the docks and at Cadoxton aggregated more than 100 miles of track. At various times the Barry company obtained or sought powers to ease the working through this congested area by means of a bypass from Weston Bridge, west of Cadoxton station, to a point on the main line north of Cadoxton Sidings, and finally by an abortive scheme of 1908 which would have given direct entry from the Cogan direction to both Cadoxton Sidings and the main line to the north of them.

In common with other South Wales railways, the Barry designated as " Up " lines those running up into the valleys; trains also ran " Up " towards Cardiff, and the Barry made a point of emphasising its moral superiority over what is now the Welsh capital by deliberately referring to " the Cardiff Branch "! To facilitate control, all its freight trains carried target numbers (as is the practice in that part of the Western Region today); thus, all trains engined by Barry shed carried the prefix B, while H1 was the first morning coal train engined from Hafod shed (Trehafod).

Between about 1900 and the First World War, the Barry employed a complex system of engine headlamp codes and coloured discs to denote the classes and routes of trains; including special passenger trains from and to the Rhymney and the B. & M. Railways, there were about twenty-five such combinations in all. Still earlier, the passenger train code included a green light to denote the Cardiff direction, and a red light to indicate Porth. Another local feature was the relatively large number of sections of line over which goods and mineral trains were authorised to travel without brake vans, or where such trains were allowed to be propelled. Permissive working of goods and empty passenger trains was

allowed under special regulations between Trehafod North–
Trehafod South, Coity Junction–Cowbridge Road Junction,
and Treforest Junction–Tonteg Junction. The double line
between the two junctions last named was not used for
regular passenger traffic in Barry Railway days, and either
line could be used if required for freight traffic in the north-
bound direction. Mineral trains starting out of Trehafod
and Treforest were frequently banked up the gradients at
the start, four of the " Yankee " 0–6–2Ts of Class K being
stationed at Hafod shed for these duties.

Passenger Trains

Considering the intensive volume of its freight traffic, and
especially the congestion of movement through the Barry
Docks area where as many as 3,650 coal wagons were
unloaded to ships in a single day, the scale of passenger
traffic operation was equally remarkable. In 1921 the
Barry–Cardiff service amounted to thirty-three trains each
way on weekdays. The Barry–Porth service, however,
never amounted to more than about half a dozen trains each
way, and that between Barry and Bridgend to a similar
figure, with a few extra short trips between Barry and
Llantwit Major. The Cardiff–Pontypridd service under-
went considerable fluctuations over the years, according to
the degree of importance which the Barry management
ascribed to competing with the Taff Vale for the through
traffic. In the summer of 1898, for example, there were ten
trains each way on this route, of which four were non-stop
between Riverside and Pontypridd in 25 minutes for the
14 miles. In the following year the service was stepped up
to twelve trains each way, none of them now being non-stop
but several being semi-fast, while even the steam railcars
which were tried on the service in 1905 ran some services
which omitted certain intermediate stops. This Barry competition for the Cardiff–Pontypridd traffic was at one time a
sufficient source of anxiety to the Taff Vale management for
them to arrange for the young son of the Pontypridd (T.V.)
station-master to be furnished each Monday morning with
cash from the booking-office till, wherewith to visit Ponty-

pridd (B.R.) station on his way to a nearby school and buy a single ticket to Cardiff. On his return from school the unused ticket was solemnly put in an envelope and forwarded to the T.V.R. head office at Queen Street, Cardiff, where the serial number of the Barry ticket was checked against that bought the previous Monday, thus enabling a continuous record to be kept of the rival concern's carryings. The Barry found difficulty in competing effectively on this route because whereas the Taff's Cardiff–Pontypridd trains served a good range of destinations beyond, the Barry trains if starting from Cardiff were not allowed to work through to the Rhondda, while traffic at the Barry intermediate stations has always been relatively light. By 1921 therefore the B.R. service had been reduced to six trains each way on weekdays, while with the development of motor traffic, the cessation of inter-railway competition, and other changes in the traffic pattern, the regular passenger service from both Cardiff and Barry to the former B.R. main line has dwindled to very small proportions since 1922. On the other hand the passenger traffic between Barry, Cardiff, and the Taff Vale and Rhymney sections beyond has been well catered for in the post-grouping period, notably by the introduction of regular interval services in the Cardiff Valleys Division in September 1953. Moreover, after the G.W.R. took over in 1922, many of the former Taff Vale trains from Cardiff via Penarth and Sully, which in pre-grouping days had been firmly kept out to the legal " frontier " at Cadoxton, were extended to Barry or Barry Island.

Apart from its regular passenger services, the Barry Railway accomplished some remarkable achievements in the handling of excursion traffic to Barry Island at summer week-ends and bank holidays. Not only was every available B.R. passenger coach and vacuum-fitted engine pressed into service, but thousands of seaside pilgrims were brought down from the valleys in trainloads of Great Western, Brecon & Merthyr, Rhymney, and even Rhondda & Swansea Bay Railway coaches. (The rival Taff Vale had its rival resort, and even its own hotel, at nearby Penarth, and it was only very rarely that its coaches were seen at Barry Island; the first occasion of which I have record was in 1908.) The

L.N.W.R. also contributed its own coaches, while in more
recent times the excursions from Tredegar were engined
throughout by " Super D " 0–8–0s fitted with tender-cabs.

The handling of up to 50,000 passengers on a bank
holiday was the more notable because until the enlargement
of the station and sidings by the G.W.R. in 1929–30, the
whole of the traffic was dealt with at two through platforms
and a terminal bay, although relief was obtained by extending some of the arriving trains empty to Barry Pier, where
the engines ran round and brought their trains back to
restart from Barry Island.

The Barry's Expresses

The Barry Railway was also notable for running two
" named trains ". One, the " Ilfracombe Boat Express ",
was a seasonal by-product of the steamboat venture: in the
summer of 1906, it left Clarence Road at 9.31 a.m. and ran
non-stop from Cardiff (G.W.) to Barry. The other was the
more famous " Ports-to-Ports Express " inaugurated by the
Great Western, Great Central, and North Eastern Railways
on 1 May 1906 between Newcastle-on-Tyne and Cardiff,
being composed of G.W. and G.C. coaches on alternate days.
One of the principal sources of business for this train was the
movement of ships' crews between South Wales and Tyne-
side, and as much of this traffic originated at Barry, the
Barry Railway persuaded the Great Western to extend the
service to Barry. It was a matter of pride for the Barry
company to insist on a B.R. engine being used for the short
run between Barry and Cardiff, where the B.R. 0–6–2T was
solemnly replaced by a G.W.R. 4–4–0. The service was
suspended during the First World War, and on its resump-
tion it was extended to Swansea via the Vale of Glamorgan
line; the schedule of 30 minutes for the 19 miles between
Barry and Bridgend was the fastest on the Barry system, and
was quite fair in relation to the gradients. For this through
working, G.W.R. 4–4–0 or 2–6–0 locomotives were used,
while in 1920 G.W.R. 2–6–2Ts of the 31XX class were
stationed at Barry shed. These engines were able to haul
heavier loads between Coity Junction and Barry than were

the B.R. o–6–2Ts, and they were also used on the nightly
through goods train between Barry and Neath, which had
been put on during the First World War. The G.W.R.
engines shared this working, also some of the Rogerstone–
Barry coal trains, with Barry o–6–4Ts and other of the
Barry's more powerful types of engine.

The " Ports-to-Ports Express " was again suspended
during the Second World War, and its present-day successor
does not run west of Cardiff.

Despite its intensive traffic, the Barry Railway had an
excellent record of safety in operation. The derailment of a
passenger train at Cogan Junction in 1893 has already been
mentioned; thereafter, only two train accidents figure in the
records of Board of Trade inquiries. Both these accidents
occurred at night, with gales blowing off the Channel: on
6 October 1904, two goods trains were in collision at
Tonteg Junction, and the driver of one was killed. Near
Barry station on the night of 4 August 1920, 2–4–2T no. 95
hauling ten six-wheeled coaches on the 10.20 p.m. passenger
train from Cardiff collided with o–6–2T no. 27, which was
shunting a cattle truck, and three passengers received minor
injuries.

Locomotives

The Barry Railway's locomotive stock exhibited the
characteristics one would expect from the nature of its origin
and traffic. A proportion of more than two locomotives per
route mile reflected high traffic density, with much trip
working and shunting, while the stock being relatively
modern developed without a single engine being scrapped
during the independent life of the company, by the end of
which there were 148 engines in all, representing seven
different wheel arrangements. All but ten engines out of the
total stock were ordered during the régime of the first locomotive superintendent (later styled Mechanical Engineer),
J. H. Hosgood, who came from the Taff Vale Railway and
held office until 1905. His successor, H. F. Golding, likewise
a former " Taff " man, continued until 1909, when John
Auld was appointed, immediately from the Glasgow & South

Western Railway, but having served previously with the Great North of Scotland and the London, Tilbury & Southend. Mr. Auld transferred to Great Western service at the 1922 amalgamation. The headquarters of the Barry locomotive, carriage, and wagon department was at Barry, where the main workshops were not fully established until 1895–7. No new engines were ever built at Barry, although some minor conversions were carried out there. The principal running sheds were also at Barry, with a small number of engines stationed out at subsidiary sheds at Hafod (Trehafod) and Coity Junction, which the G.W.R. closed after grouping. The Barry Railway also had the right to use the Brecon & Merthyr's engine shed at Rhymney, but in practice no Barry engines were stationed there as the workings up the B. & M. Extension were based on Barry shed.

For what was primarily a mineral line, the Barry engines were very smartly turned out, especially in Mr. Golding's time. The basic livery was " crimson-chocolate " with black border and vermilion lining, the buffer beams being vermilion with black border and white lining, and the company's initials being lettered in gold with blue shading. All classes of tank locomotives except Auld's 0–6–4Ts, which were the final Barry design, displayed the engine number in brass lettering on the front of the chimney and on the back of the coal bunker, while at various times there were three different varieties of brass number-plate on the tanks or cab-sides exhibiting the company's name in addition to the engine number. Auld's 0–6–4Ts carried the front number on the smokebox door. Latterly most engines displayed a transfer of the armorial insignia, as well as the " B.R." monogram within a garter, while the four-coupled passenger tank engines sported highly polished brass domes and copper caps to the chimneys. Until the panelling and lining had to be modified in the First World War, there was thus very little risk of anybody on Cardiff station mistaking a Barry engine for either a Great Western or a Taff Vale one!

For all this exterior bravura, the Barry however maintained a rugged simplicity in certain directions. Only four engines, for example, were fitted with steam heating connections, these being the 2–4–2 Ts nos. 21 and 22, and later two of the 0–6–2Ts, nos. 38 and 43. The two four-coupled engines were so fitted for working the saloons, or for warming the coaches of the Barry–Newcastle express while standing in the bay platform at Barry, while the two 0–6–2Ts were those which normally worked the same train between Barry and Cardiff. Classes of engine equipped with the combined steam-and-vacuum brake comprised all the four-coupled passenger types, the 0–6–4Ts, and some of the 0–6–2Ts of Classes B and B1. Early photographs show some of the Class A 0–6–0Ts similarly equipped, since at the outset of operations these were the only engines available for working passenger trains, but when more suitable power became available the vacuum connections were removed. Four 0–6–2Ts, nos. 60, 108, 111, and 122, were fitted with the Westinghouse brake for working special trains of Rhymney Railway stock.

Until he was forced by the saturation of home manufacturing capacity temporarily to " buy foreign ", Mr. Hosgood was able from the start to maintain a high degree of standardisation, so that the same design of boiler sufficed for five of the types which he introduced. The main source of supply was Sharp, Stewart & Co., who with their successors, the North British Locomotive Company, supplied in all 102 of the 150 engines built for the Barry Railway. The original Classes A (five engines) and B (twenty-five engines) of 1888—90 were conventional inside-cylinder 0–6–0 and 0–6–2 side tank designs respectively, of a general pattern very popular and useful among the South Wales railways. Class A was not expanded beyond the original five engines but the dimensions formed the basis of Class F introduced between 1890 and 1905, and fitted with saddle tanks instead of side tanks for greater adhesion; this very useful class eventually numbered twenty-eight engines. Six of them were loaned to the G.W.R. in 1917, and were stationed mainly at Neath, Port Talbot, and Newport. The B1 Class of 0–6–2Ts (forty-two engines) also introduced in 1890 was generally similar to the B Class, except for slightly longer frames and increased tank capacity; owing to the inability of British manufacturers to supply, the last five engines of this class (nos. 122–126) were built in 1899–1900 by the S. A.

D

Franco-Belge of Liége. No. 126 of this series was exhibited at the Paris Exhibition in 1900. Mr. Hosgood had to go even further afield for the final design of Barry 0–6–2T, the five engines nos. 117–121 which comprised Class K being obtained in 1899 from the Cooke Locomotive Works of Paterson, New Jersey. These " Yankees " were the only six-coupled engines built for the Barry with outside cylinders, and the boilers were slightly larger than those of Classes B and F. The valve-gear was of American pattern, while another unusual feature was the combined bar-and-plate frames, the bar frame extending to the back of the firebox where it was joined to an orthodox rear plate frame. Some at least of these engines as delivered also had American type smokebox doors, only half the diameter of the smokebox itself, but these were replaced with full-size doors. Vacuum brake pipes were also fitted originally, but were later removed. All the American boilers were replaced during 1909–11 by Barry standard boilers.

All the 0–6–2T classes shared in the working of mineral trains, while Classes A and F especially undertook much of the trip working to and from the docks and shunting at the coal tips and in Cadoxton Sidings. The only other type of six-coupled tank engine not yet mentioned under the Hosgood régime comprised the five small 0–6–0T shunters of Class E, nos. 33, 34, 50, 51 and 53, built by Hudswell, Clarke & Co. in 1889–91. Their normal role was to shunt various sidings in the docks area having restricted curves or clearances, but they had two spells of more exalted duty, once in working trains over the temporary diversion in Porthkerry Park, and again from 1909 onwards, when nos. 33 and 53 were converted for auto-train working, coupled to one four-wheeled and one six-wheeled coach. This was in Mr. Golding's time, and he caused the little engines from the docks to blossom out with polished domes, coats-of-arms and, in the case of no. 33, a copper-capped chimney also.

The object of this conversion was to reinforce two steam railcars, separately numbered 1 and 2, which in accordance with contemporary fashion the Barry company had ordered in 1904 from the North British Locomotive Company,

Glasgow, who delivered them early in 1905. There were 64 ft. 10 in. long overall and were mounted on two four-wheeled bogies, one of which carried the vertical boiler supplying steam at 160 lb. per sq. in. to two 12 by 16 in. cylinders. Total seating accommodation was only ten first class and forty third class, so that their range of use was distinctly limited. They were first tried on the Cardiff–Pontypridd service, but were sorely tried in another sense by the curved 1 in 89 climb from St. Fagan's up to Tynycaeau. They then gravitated to the Vale of Glamorgan line, working short trips in the summer especially between Barry and Llantwit Major. With the coming of the auto-trains in 1909, the use of the railcars fluctuated greatly; they spent a good deal of time resting in the shed which had been specially built for them alongside the carriage sheds at Barry, but were nevertheless in great demand for extra trips between Cadoxton, Barry, and the Island at holiday week-ends, when trains from Cardiff or Pontypridd arrived too full to clear the local traffic. They were withdrawn altogether in 1913, being denuded of their motive units and converted into a two-coach gangwayed set, known as " the Vestibule Train ". The Barry enginemen were not sorry at their disappearance, because coaling had to be performed a bucketful at a time, through a sliding door, while the smallest boy cleaner at Barry shed had to crawl into the tiny firebox to carry out the daily tube-cleaning, and, so it is alleged, could only squeeze through if he removed all or most of his clothes! In 1906 the Barry directors ordered designs to be prepared for Railcars 3 and 4 with a view to working a regular service to Caerphilly, but this idea was dropped.

The First 0–8–0 in Britain

While the Barry shared with its neighbours, the Taff Vale and the Rhymney Railways, the distinction of employing a few tender engines on relatively short-distance coal traffic, its venture into this field of design was wholly fortuitous, albeit it conferred upon this Welsh company the distinction of being the first in Britain to use eight-coupled tender

D*

locomotives.   This came about because in 1889 Messrs. Sharp, Stewart had on their hands some outside-cylindered 0–8–0s with four-wheeled tenders, built for the Swedish & Norwegian Railway, which had found itself unable to pay for them.   The Barry bought two of them as nos. 35 and 36 in 1889, and two more in 1897 which became B.R. 92 and 93, making up Class D.   Being tender engines their use was rather restricted, but after the opening of the B. & M. Extension they proved very useful on the heavy coal trains from the McLaren Collieries in the Rhymney Valley.

Having thus pioneered the introduction of the 0–8–0 tender type, Hosgood went one better in 1896 with his Class H, comprising seven engines, nos. 79–85.   These were 0–8–2 side tanks with outside cylinders, being the first engines to have this wheel arrangement in Great Britain.   Neither Hosgood nor his successors continued the eight-wheels-coupled trend, however, but Auld in his solitary design turned to yet another different wheel arrangement, the 0–6–4T.   Ten locomotives of this type, nos. 139–148 of Class L, were built by Hawthorn, Leslie's in 1914, and shared the heaviest coal train working on the main line with the eight-coupled engines.   There was not a great deal to choose between the haulage capacity of these principal types; in 1921 both eight-coupled Classes D and H were expected to take sixty-five empties Up or seventy loaded mineral wagons Down the main line to or from Trehafod, and Class L, sixty-three each way.   Over the B. & M. Extension, the loadings of the eight-coupled classes were reduced by five wagons each way, but the 0–6–4Ts took the same loads as over the main line.

Passenger Engines

Of Barry locomotives built solely for passenger traffic, the first were four small 2–4–0Ts (Class C) of Sharp, Stewart's standard design of the period: nos. 21 and 22 were built in 1889, and 37 and 52 in the following year.   With the object of increasing their adhesion and bunker capacity, Hosgood converted nos. 52, 22 and 21 to 2–4–2T in 1898,

1901 and 1903 respectively, but in 1898 nos. 37 and 52 were sold to the Port Talbot Railway & Dock Company, whose locomotive affairs were in the hands of Mr. Hosgood's brother. No. 37 finished her days as a 2–4–0T, and by conveniently leaving some numbers blank in their stock, the Port Talbot company saved themselves the bother of changing her number.

With the rapid growth of passenger traffic, two further classes, G and J, were provided for this purpose. The former comprised four 0–4–4Ts, two built in 1892 and two more in 1895; they were handsome machines whose design had much in common with those of the S.E. & C.R. and other railways. They worked largely on the main line to Pontypridd. In 1897, Hosgood reverted to the 2–4–2T wheel arrangement with the class J design, of which the first three came from Hudswell, Clarke in that year; three more from Sharp, Stewart in 1898; and a final five from the same stable in 1899. Allowing for repairs, these seventeen four-coupled engines were barely sufficient for the ordinary passenger services, and were reinforced by 0–6–2Ts as required; at summer weekends, anything fitted with the vacuum brake apparatus would be turned out.

Thus the total locomotive stock of the Barry Railway at the end of the company's life amounted to 148 engines, comprising: 0–8–0 tender, 4; 0–8–2T, 7; 0–6–4T, 10; 0–6–2T, 72; 0–6–0T, 38; 0–4–4T, 4; and 2–4–2T, 13. After the amalgamation with the G.W.R. in 1922, the slump in the coal shipping trade rendered much of the South Wales motive power redundant, and at the end of ten years of grouping, just over one-third of the Barry locomotives had been withdrawn. As with other South Wales railways, however, much interesting modification of Barry engines was carried out by the substitution of Great Western type cabs, boiler fittings and bunkers, and in some cases coned boilers. As an extreme example, eleven of the class F saddle-tanks were rebuilt as pannier tanks. Two of the American-built 0–6–2Ts were reconstructed with coned boilers, and a start was also made on similar rebuilding of the 0–6–4Ts, but the whole of this last-named class was summarily withdrawn in the latter part of 1926. These engines had been fitted

originally with the vacuum brake, but the propensity to
unsteadiness which seems to have been inherent in this wheel
arrangement on various British railways caused their removal
from passenger work, while a tendency to derailment on
some of the sharply curved Barry Sidings hastened their
eventual withdrawal. Of the 148 Barry engines which
passed into Great Western stock, twenty-six survived into
the British Railways régime in 1948, the last survivors under
nationalisation being the class B1 0–6–2T nos. 270, 271, 274
and 276, which were all withdrawn in April 1951. No. 258,
although withdrawn in 1949, survived as a Works pilot at
Swindon until May 1953. Thereafter, examples of Barry
locomotive practice still survived in industrial use in various
parts of the country, a number of Barry engines—including
no fewer than twenty-two of the Class F engines—having
been sold to collieries and other industrial users. Almost the
last link with the locomotive history of the Barry Railway
was severed in December 1959, when the repair of locomotives was discontinued at Barry and both the locomotive
and carriage shops were given over to the repair of wagons.
But, by the introduction into Britain of the 0–8–0 tender and
0–8–2T wheel arrangements, by the density of its locomotive
population in relation to size of system, and by the splendour
of the livery, the Barry Railway had not failed to leave its
modest impress upon British locomotive history.

Coaching Stock

The Barry coaching stock presented curious contrasts
between the primitive and the modern. All the passenger
vehicles were built with or converted to electric lighting, but
not even the most modern had steam heat or communication
cords, while a large proportion of the third class compartments were devoid of upholstery and had wooden slatted
seats of tramcar pattern for the use of colliers and dockers.
The earliest vehicles, built in 1888–90 by the Metropolitan
Carriage & Wagon Company, were all four-wheeled and of
three main types: a third class of five compartments, a composite of two first and two second compartments, and a
brake van; there were respectively twenty, eight, and eight

vehicles of these three types, and the brake vans originally had a single third class passenger compartment. With the growth of passenger traffic, more commodious six-wheeled coaches were introduced between 1893 and 1900, and these followed the same general pattern in comprising sixty-nine thirds of six compartments each, nineteen composites of two firsts and three seconds each, and twenty-two brakes each having one third class compartment. The orders for these were spread among four different builders: Gloucester Carriage & Wagon, Ashburys, Oldbury Carriage & Wagon, and Brown & Marshall. The last three named firms were merged with the Metropolitan C. & W. Company to become the Metropolitan Amalgamated C. & W. Co. in 1902, this last in turn being absorbed in the Metropolitan Cammell Company. In 1916 the Barry added substantially to its coaching fleet by opportune purchases of second-hand Lancashire & Yorkshire six-wheelers of various types: sixteen thirds, six composite first and second, and eight brake thirds, of which five had " balloon ends " with raised roofs over the guard's lookout. These L. & Y. coaches made up four train-sets, two of ten coaches and two of five coaches.

The fleet of coaches just described sufficed the Barry Railway until after the First World War, when two very modern train-sets, each composed of seven non-corridor bogie coaches, were ordered from the Birmingham Railway Carriage & Wagon Company and delivered in 1920; they were designed in the drawing office at Barry, but unkind critics averred that their design owed quite a lot to the activities of various Barry officials who were observed to be very busy with notebooks and tape-measures whenever a foreign company's bogie coaches worked into Barry on special trains! The new trains were nicknamed the " Marble Arch " sets because of their high rounded roofs; each set consisted of two brake thirds, three thirds, and two tri-composites; the last named were remarkable vehicles containing four second class and three first class compartments, and a single third class at one end. The basic livery of Barry coaching stock was a reddish or lake colour, generally similar to that of the engines; except during Mr. Golding's régime, class designations were not shown in words but in large gold letters on the carriage doors.

As to other coaching vehicles, the directors' saloon was an impressive-looking bogie affair with clerestory roof, built by Craven's in 1899. There was a more utilitarian officers' inspection carriage on six wheels, with verandah ends, but the star turn among Barry departmental vehicles was the pay clerks' van, which was officially recorded as having begun life in 1890 as mineral brake van no. 31. It had an intermediate existence as the " Manager's Truck ", in which capacity it was hauled about by 2–4–0T no. 21, and was reputed to be in seasonal demand for picnics and shooting parties also. A short time after the first general manager, Richard Evans, retired in 1905 it was fitted with a 40 h.p. petrol motor in emulation of similar experiments on other railways elsewhere, and presumably with a view also to expediting the movements of the pay clerks from station to station in the best Wells Fargo manner. Failures of the petrol motor were both frequent and ignominious, however, and the self-propelled pay clerks soon reverted to the more conservative care of no. 21.

Freight Rolling Stock

Although practically the whole of the coal traffic was conveyed in private owners' wagons (all of which had to be re-sorted at Barry or Cadoxton and returned to the right colliery), the company by the end of its life nevertheless had 1,563 freight vehicles, apart from 573 service vehicles. This relatively large number was due to the need to provide for import traffic from Barry Docks, including substantial quantities of flour and timber. The company only had two carriage trucks, however, and when a circus or fair was being moved from Barry Island to Porthcawl, Aberavon, or the Rhondda, special vehicles had to be borrowed, usually from the Great Western. However, those were leisurely days, and nobody seemed to worry much when the move of a fair from the Island to Ferndale had to be spread over five days.

The Barry had over seventy mineral brake vans, of which the two earlier types were four-wheeled and weighed 7 and

11 tons respectively, while the third version, introduced in 1915, was six-wheeled and scaled 20 tons tare. Most if not all of the brake vans were vacuum-piped, to enable them to be attached to passenger trains when required. This came in useful when working the last passenger train of the day, the engine being able to draw off the brake van at, say, Pontypridd or Bridgend, and forthwith to pick up a coal train.

Like most of the independent South Wales railways, the Barry used lower-quadrant somersault signals, but with the additional feature in many cases of double white stripes on the front of the semaphore and double black stripes on the back. One stripe was placed towards the outer edge of the arm, and the other near the post: in the case of distant signals, the effect of the two white "fishtail" stripes was most unusual. In latter days, the semaphores were made of pressed steel and enamelled. Some examples of B.R. somersault signals were still in use in May 1961.

As regards signal-box equipment, down to 1903 all or most of the mechanical locking frames were of the Saxby & Farmer type. The first signal-box for which an order was placed on Saxby's was in 1887 for Cadoxton Junction (at that time forty-one levers), and was for an interim design between the cam-and-rocker Saxby frame which was standard on the London, Brighton & South Coast Railway and the Saxby-Duplex-Plunger type of 1888. The latter type was used for the majority of the larger Barry frames, the last of this type of mechanical locking to be installed being Barry Dock Low Level Junction (forty-five levers) in 1890. Thereafter a curious thing happened; about the turn of the century Saxby's had absorbed the Chippenham signalling firm of Evans O'Donnell, and Saxby's then started to supply Evans O'Donnell frames for the Barry Railway and continued to do so right down to 1921. The largest of these frames was the ninety-lever replacement of Barry Island Junction Box in 1907.*

---

* For research and information into the history of these locking frames, the author is indebted to Mr. O. S. Nock, Chief Mechanical Engineer, Signal & Colliery Division, Westinghouse Brake & Signal Co. Ltd.

Contracting for equipment at outlying places on Welsh railways was not without its humorous side, albeit often perplexing in its consequences to the research student of later years. The Barry's extension to the Brecon & Merthyr called for a small intermediate signal-box between Penrhos and Energlyn Junctions at a place called Gwaun Gledyr. Now, the Rhymney Railway was intending to build a branch from the Caerphilly direction towards Gwaun Gledyr, so either to avoid confusion, or merely on the grounds of being different, the Barry dropped the two initial G's and called its box " Waenledyr ". All this Welsh euphony and euphemism must have been too much for the gentleman who came from Chippenham to reconnoitre the site and book the order, and who one imagines trying to decipher the rain-sodden pages of his notebook after tramping the long grass from Penrhos to Energlyn under the guidance of some very loquacious Welsh cicerone, in one of the Principality's more protracted and penetrative drizzles. So " Waenledyr " went down in the order book as " Red Meadow ", which at least sounds vaguely similar if in fact it means something quite different; one can only regret that this extremely free interpreter of the Welsh language was never given the opportunity to produce his own version of Tynycaeau Junction.

Results of the Grouping

Coinciding as it did with the post-war decline in coal exports, the introduction of a single management for the G.W.R. and its newly amalgamated companies in South Wales naturally led to a progressive reduction in formerly competitive facilities. Since most of the collieries were more directly served by older routes, the former Barry system suffered particularly in this process. A first step was the introduction of through engine-workings, largely with G.W.R. eight-coupled tank engines, between Cadoxton and the Rhondda collieries, enabling much of the marshalling and engine-changing at Trehafod to be cut out, and the Barry engine-shed there was closed early in 1926. In the same year the G.W.R. took powers by its Act of 4 August 1926 to abandon the whole of the B. & M. Extension Line between Penrhos Lower Junction and Barry Junction (B. & M.); traffic for Barry was diverted via the Rhymney section and Penrhos Upper Junction, but it was not until 1937 that the last of the three viaducts on the B. & M. Extension was finally demolished. Meanwhile, traffic over the Barry main line to the Rhondda had been further reduced, and the opening of a new connection between the B.R. and Taff Vale sections at Tonteg Junction enabled the Barry–Porth passenger service to be diverted through the ex-T.V.R. stations at Treforest and Pontypridd, and the former B.R. stations at those places to be closed on and from 10 July 1930. In 1943, the Barry Up line between Tonteg and Pwllgwaun was closed as a running road and used for storage; this part of the main line was closed entirely for through traffic in June 1951. The 1¼ miles at the Rhondda end between Trehafod and Pwllgwaun signal-box remained in use until 1956 to serve Maesycoed goods depot, which had been opened in 1907 and was finally closed on and from 4 July 1956. The historic connection between the Barry and the Taff Vale at Trehafod was taken out, and the bridge over the River Taff dismantled, about two years later.

Rundown continued until in 1978 the only part of the former Barry Railway system still in use (excluding dock lines and the former Vale of Glamorgan Railway) comprised rather less than seven miles between Barry Island and the junction at Cogan with the former Taff Vale Railway.

Local passenger services between Barry, Cadoxton and Pontypridd, also betweeen Cardiff and Pontypridd via St Fagan's, were withdrawn on 10 September 1962. In the following year the connection between Drope Junction (Barry Railway) and the former G.W.R. main line at Peterston was closed on 1 March, while the destruction by fire of Tynycaeau North signal box later in the same month led to the cessation of freight traffic to Barry via Walnut Tree Viaduct and T.C. Junction on 30 March 1963. The main line between Cadoxton Yard (North) and Tonteg Junction was closed on 17 June of the same year, traffic for

Barry being diverted via Radyr and Cogan. Communication with the dolomite siding at Walnut Tree West
continued to be available from Penrhos Junction across the
Walnut Tree Viaduct, however, until 14 December 1967,
the girders of the great bridge being removed in 1969, and
the masonry piers finally demolished in 1973.

Since the closure of the Barry main line the site of
Cadoxton Junction and the once busy yards beyond have
been built over, while the nearby site of Biglis Junction with
the former Taff Vale Railway's coast line from Penarth
became derelict after the passenger service on this route was
withdrawn on 6 May 1968. The Barry's branch between
Barry Island and Barry Pier seems not to have been used
after the last call there of the steamer *Balmoral* in October
1971, but was not officially closed until 5 July 1976.

Barry and Barry Island stations are now served by a
frequent service of diesel multiple-unit trains, basically to
and from Merthyr, integrating at Cardiff Central (so
renamed in 1966) with services to and from the Valleys.
Longer-distance excursions are still frequently run to Barry
or Barry Island, though enthusiasts for whom the dwindling
graveyard of BR steam locos is still an attraction can no
longer enjoy the sigh of Westinghouse pumps on Rhymney
Railway locomotives, nor the sight of an ex-L.N.W.R.
0–8–0 being turned on the triangle in the dock lines area
near Barry Town!

Vale of Glamorgan

The Vale of Glamorgan line lost its local passenger
service between Barry and Bridgend on 15 June 1964, the
intermediate stations being closed for freight traffic (other
than some private sidings) at various times between
1961–67. The route is still used when required for passenger
diversions—H.S.T's and all—when the main line between
Cardiff and Bridgend is temporarily closed for engineering
work. The Vale is also busy with block freight train traffic,

notably up to 100 coal trains weekly from various collieries and other despatch points in South Wales to the C.E.G.B. generating station at Aberthaw, with an extensive rail layout equipped for handling "merry-go-round" (M.G.R.) traffic. An important addition to the freight traffic on the V.o.G. line occurred from the opening on 15 January 1980 of a short branch from near Ewenny, S.E. of Bridgend, to serve the Ford Motor Company's Engine Factory.

The former Bridgend Avoiding Line between Cowbridge Road and Coity Junctions was closed on 15 June 1964, except for a short connection from Coity Junction at the northern end down to Bridgend Coity depot, which in 1982 was still open for occasional coal trains from Margam.

Barry Docks

Ownership and management of Barry Docks, which between 1922–47 had lain with G.W.R., passed after nationalisation to the British Transport Commission (B.T.C.), but with the abolition of this latter body under the Transport Act 1962, became the responsibility of the British Transport Docks Board (B.T.D.B.). Despite the long decline of the traditional coal trade, Barry Docks still have an export trade in fuel, sixty years after the Barry Railway Company ceased to exist; in 1978 the B.T.D.B.—which has continued like its predecessors to develop general cargo trade through South Wales ports—installed at Barry No 2 Dock a conveyor system for loading railborne or roadborne bulk cargo. In 1981 this system handled 93,000 tonnes of railborne export coke, together with 25,000 tons of Phurnacite patent fuel from Abercwmboi. In 1982 the rail traffic from South Wales coke ovens was expected to be 30,000 tonnes up on 1981, destined for Roumania.

Many of the Barry Railway stations embodied well-proportioned, twin-gabled brick buildings, ornamented by the initials "BR" on one gable and the date on the other—a combination which will probably mislead archaeologists of future centuries into learned controversy as to whether their history books are wrong in claiming that British Railways came into being in 1948! Barry station itself however had only timber buildings until 28 March 1955, when the present station was formally opened.

The Barry Dock & Railway will never rank among the physical giants in British railway history, but its significance eclipsed its size. It was perhaps the last British railway system to be constructed that was outstandingly successful: the ultimate and richest nugget to come from the dark Eldorado that was the South Wales coalfield in the nineteenth century. It ranked with Dowlais Ironworks and with the Ocean Collieries as examples of what could be accomplished in an astonishingly short time by men of wealth, purpose, and determination; if there was such a thing as "the Railway Age", then the Barry must be counted among its landmarks. For the student of railway history, research into its story discloses a far greater treasure-house of enterprise, anecdote, and incident than can be compressed into this short sketch.

(Acknowledgements for help in this revision to Mr. E. R. Mountford, to British Rail (Western Region, Cardiff) and to British Transport Docks Board.)

Appendix I

LOCOMOTIVES OF THE BARRY RAILWAY

(ST—Saddle tank; OC—Outside cylinders)

Barry Rly. Nos.	Class	Wheel Arrangement	Builders	Date	Works Nos.	Remarks
1–5	A	0-6-0T	Sharp, Stewart	1888	3449–53	—
6–10	B	0-6-2T	Sharp, Stewart	1888	3454–58	—
11–20	B	0-6-2T	Sharp, Stewart	1888	3459–68	—
21, 22	C	2-4-0T	Sharp, Stewart	1889	3528–29	22 converted to 2-4-2T 1901; 21 converted to 2-4-2T 1903
23–25	B	0-6-2T	Sharp, Stewart	1889	3571–73	—
26–32	B	0-6-2T	Sharp, Stewart	1890	3574–80	—
33–34	E	0-6-0T	Hudswell, Clarke	1889	331–32	33 ran for a time as 0-4-2T; see main text.
35–36	D	0-8-0	Sharp, Stewart	1889	3446–47	Purchased 1889. OC.
37	C	2-4-0T	Sharp, Stewart	1889	3610	Sold to P.T.R. & D. Co., 1898.
37	F	0-6-0ST	Sharp, Stewart	1900	4593	Took number of previous no. 37, see above.
38–46	B1	0-6-2T	Sharp, Stewart	1890	3598–3606	—
47–49	F	0-6-0ST	Sharp, Stewart	1900	3607–09	—
50–51	E	0-6-0ST	Hudswell, Clarke	1900	343, 344	—
52	C	2-4-0T	Sharp, Stewart	1900	3626	Rebuilt as 2-4-2T in 1898 for P.T.R. & D. Co.
52	F	0-6-0ST	Sharp, Stewart	1900	4594	Took no. of previous no. 52; see above.
53	E	0-6-0T	Hudswell, Clarke	1891	352	Ran temporarily as 0-4-2T.
54–63	B1	0-6-2T	Vulcan Foundry	1892	1336–45	—
64, 65	F	0-6-0ST	Vulcan Foundry	1892	1346–47	—
66, 67	G	0-4-4T	Vulcan Foundry	1892	1348–49	—
68, 69	G	0-4-4T	Sharp, Stewart	1895	4053–54	—
70–72	F	0-6-0ST	Sharp, Stewart	1894	4050–52	—
73–78	B1	0-6-2T	Sharp, Stewart	1894	4044–49	—
79–85	H	0-8-2T	Sharp, Stewart	1896	4182–88	OC.
86–88	E	0-6-0T	Hudswell, Clarke	1897	473–475	—
89–91	J	2-4-2T	Sharp, Stewart	1898	4367–69	—
92	D	0-8-0	Sharp, Stewart	1886	3365	OC. Purchased 1897
93	D	0-8-0	Sharp, Stewart	1887	3394	OC. Purchased 1897
94–98	J	2-4-2T	Sharp, Stewart	1899	4497–4501	—
99–104	F	0-6-0ST	Sharp, Stewart	1900	4595–4600	—
105–116	B1	0-6-2T	Sharp, Stewart	1900	4607–18	—
117–121	K	0-6-2T	Cooke Loco Works	1899	2483–86 (See 'Remarks')	OC. No. 117 had works no. 2484, 118/2482, 119/2483, 120/2485, 121/2486.
122–126	B1	0-6-2T	S.A. Franco-Belge	1900	1272–76	—
127–132	F	0-6-0ST	North British Loco Co.	1905	16628–33	—
133–138	F	0-6-2T	Hudswell, Clarke	1905	712–717	—
139–148	L	0-6-4T	Hawthorn, Leslie	1914	3038–47	—

Appendix II

RENUMBERING OF BARRY RAILWAY ENGINES
IN G.W.R. STOCK, 1922

Barry Nos.	G.W.R. Nos.	Barry Nos.	G.W.R. Nos.
1, 2	599, 700	69	9
3, 4	702, 703	70–72	716–718
5	706	73–78	255–260
6–9	198–201	79–85	1380–1386
10, 11	203, 204	86–91	1311–1316
12–20	206–214	92, 93	1389, 1390
21, 22	1322, 1323	94–98	1317–1321
23–32	223–232	99–104	719–724
33, 34	781, 782	105–116	261–272
35, 36	1387, 1388	117–121	193–197
37	708	122–126	273–277
38–40	233–235	127, 128	725, 726
41	238	129	807
42–46	240–244	130	729
47–49	710–712	131	742
50, 51	783, 784	132	747
52	713	133	754
53	785	134–138	776–780
54–63	245–254	139–147	1347–1355
64, 65	714, 715	148	1357
66–68	2–4		

Appendix III

LOCOMOTIVES OF THE BARRY RAILWAY

Leading Dimensions of Principal Classes, as Built

Class(es)	Coupled Wheels diameter	Cylinders (ins.)	Boiler Pressure (lb./sq. in.)
A, B, B1, F	4′ 3″	18 × 26	150
C	5′ 3″	17 × 24	150
D	4′ 3″	20 × 26	150
E	3′ 3½″	14 × 20	140
G	5′ 7½″	18 × 26	150
H	4′ 3″	20 × 26	150
J	5′ 7½″	18 × 26	150
K	4′ 3″	18 × 24	160
L	4′ 7″	18½ × 26	180

(Note:—One standard class of boiler was suitable for Classes A, B, B1, F, G, and J as built, and
also for Class K when reboilered.)

AUTHORITIES

Unlike other of the South Wales railways, the history of the Barry Railway is well documented. In 1923, a memorial *History of the Barry Railway Company, 1884–1921*, by R. J. Rimell (sometime assistant secretary of the company) in association with Messrs. Davies and Hailey, was published by *The Western Mail*, Cardiff, while many references to David Davies's associations with the promotion and opening are to be found in *Top Sawyer* (A Biography of David Davies of Llandinam) by Ivor Thomas (Longmans, Green & Co., 1938). These and other authorities deal mainly with the commercial and docks aspects of the undertaking, however, whereas the present book is intended to concentrate upon the " railway " side, in conformity with the general pattern of the Oakwood Library of Railway History. This book is based mainly upon the archives of the Barry Company as preserved by the British Transport Commission, but acknowledgment is also made to the following other sources:

E. L. Chappell, *History of the Port of Cardiff* (Cardiff, Priory Press, 1939).

C. S. Howells, *Transport Facilities in S. Wales & Monmouthshire* (University College of S. Wales & Monmouthshire, 1911).

E. D. Lewis, *The Rhondda Valleys* (London, Phoenix House, 1959).

G. E. Farr, *West Country Passenger Steamers* (London, Richard Tilling, 1956).

Duckworth & Langmuir, *Railway and Other Steamers* (Glasgow, Shipping Histories, Ltd., 1948).

R. H. Edwards, " Some Historical Notes on the Docks in South Wales " (Proc. S. Wales & Monmouthshire Railways & Docks Lecture & Debating Society, 1957).

T. B. Sands, " Some Railway Byways in S. Wales " (Paper read to Railway Club, 1951).

E. L. Ahrons, *Locomotive and Train Working in the Latter Part of the 19th Century* (Railway Magazine, 1923; republished in series ed. L. L. Asher, Heffer & Sons, Cambridge, 1953).

Periodicals

The Locomotive (series, 1923).

The Railway Magazine, notably October 1906 (Illustrated interviews), March 1907, and April 1918 (H. L. Hopwood).

Great Western Railway Magazine (XXXIV, No. 7, July 1922).

Model Railway News (December, 1955); *Railway Observer; Railway Times; Railway News; Railway Gazette; Railway Year Book; Bradshaw; South Wales Daily News; South Wales Argus; Western Mail; Cardiff Evening Express.*

ACKNOWLEDGMENTS

The author acknowledges with gratitude the help generously provided in making available sources of material, or in checking particular inquiries, by the Archivist, British Transport Commission; the General Manager and officers of the Western Region, British Railways; the General Manager, British Transport Docks; the Hon. Librarian of the Railway Club; Cardiff Central Library; and (for information and drawings, etc., of rolling-stock) the Birmingham Railway Carriage & Wagon Co. Ltd., the Metropolitan-Cammell Carriage & Wagon Co. Ltd., and the North British Locomotive Company, Ltd.

Among a large number of friends who have helped personally with information and research he would mention particularly the continuous and enthusiastic assistance over several years of Mr. E. R. Mountford of Caerphilly, who also read the MS. and proofs; also Messrs. C. R. Clinker, the late George Daniel, J. M. Dunn, Miss A. H. Ferguson, and Messrs. M. D. Greville, C. W. Harris, Trefor L. Jones, Charles E. Lee, Michael Linsey, Rev. W. T. Phillips, R. C. Riley, R. M. Robbins, T. B. Sands, and B. G. Wilson.

Acknowledgments are made for permission to reproduce photographs as follows: Birmingham Railway Carriage & Wagon Co., 76; British Transport Commission, 50, 52; Western Region, British Railways, 51, 57; South Wales Docks, 56; W. A. Camwell collection, 53; V. C. Hardacre, 54; B. W. Mills, 62, 65; Locomotive Publishing Co., 61, 64, 67–71, 73–5; E. R. Mountford, 77, 79; North British Locomotive Co., 78; J. Pitt, 72; H. J. Patterson Rutherford, 58–60; C. Farmer, 80. Nos. 55, 63, and 66 are from the author's collection.